THE UNIVERSITY OF NORTH CAROLINA
SESQUICENTENNIAL PUBLICATIONS

PIONEERING A PEOPLE'S THEATRE

THE UNIVERSITY OF NORTH CAROLINA
SESQUICENTENNIAL PUBLICATIONS

*Louis R. Wilson,* **Director**


CHRONICLES OF THE SESQUICENTENNIAL

THE UNIVERSITY OF NORTH CAROLINA, 1789-1835
*A Documentary History*

THE CAMPUS OF THE FIRST STATE UNIVERSITY

THE GRADUATE SCHOOL: RESEARCH AND PUBLICATIONS

THE GRADUATE SCHOOL: DISSERTATIONS AND THESES

STUDIES IN SCIENCE

STUDIES IN LANGUAGE AND LITERATURE

A HUNDRED YEARS OF LEGAL EDUCATION

A STATE UNIVERSITY SURVEYS THE HUMANITIES

SECONDARY EDUCATION IN THE SOUTH

IN SEARCH OF THE REGIONAL BALANCE OF AMERICA

STUDIES IN HISTORY AND POLITICAL SCIENCE

LIBRARY RESOURCES OF THE UNIVERSITY OF NORTH CAROLINA

RESEARCH AND REGIONAL WELFARE

PIONEERING A PEOPLE'S THEATRE

UNIVERSITY EXTENSION IN ACTION

BOOKS FROM CHAPEL HILL

# PIONEERING
# A PEOPLE'S THEATRE

*Edited with a Foreword by*

ARCHIBALD HENDERSON
KENAN PROFESSOR OF MATHEMATICS

CHAPEL HILL
THE UNIVERSITY OF NORTH CAROLINA PRESS
1945

*Copyright,* 1945, by
The Carolina Playmakers

# Foreword

## By ARCHIBALD HENDERSON

OVER a period of somewhat more than a quarter of a century, an organization for the furtherance of the arts of the drama and the theatre, known as The Carolina Playmakers, has flourished here under the leadership of its founder, the late Frederick Henry Koch. During this period, 1919-1945, upwards of four thousand students have joined the organization and participated in its activities; and hundreds of thousands of people have attended the indoor and outdoor productions and listened in on the radio broadcasts, of plays, original and classic, light and serious, farce, comedy, tragedy, tragi-comedy, pageants, and historical dramas. The stimulating influence of this preoccupation with the drama and the theatre, which rapidly pervaded North Carolina and the Southeastern area, eventually spread throughout the entire country and into Canada, and focused attention upon Chapel Hill as a radiating center of inspiration and as a beacon light to the younger generation.

*Pioneering a People's Theatre* has appeared as Vol. XVII, No. 1, of *The Carolina Play-Book*. It is singularly appropriate that a volume which serves both as a memorial to Koch and as a survey, summary, and appraisal of the labors and accomplishments of The Carolina Playmakers, should appear during the culminating year of the Sesquicentennial Celebration of the University of North Carolina and be included in the Sesquicentennial Publications of the University. It follows soon upon the passing of that vivid and perennially youthful spirit—reminiscent of Milton's friend drowned in 1637:

> For Lycidas is dead, dead ere his prime,
> Young Lycidas, and hath not left his peer.

This volume, without pretension to be either formal history or complete record, presents a cross section of the life and growth of The Carolina Playmakers. Here are highlights, actors, interpreters, scenery, background—the essentials of a true drama in the educational history of the Nation. Koch presents the ideology of folk playmaking; Selden, the able new leader, of-

## PIONEERING A PEOPLE'S THEATRE

fers a thoughtful appraisal and lucid estimate, both of Koch the personality, player, and sower of dreams, and of the place of dramatic arts in the University curriculum. In vivid strokes are portrayed the original and authentically American contributions of Koch to the American drama and theatre: the meaning and inspiration of the "folkplay" and the democratic technic of critically moulding the creative product. In his inimitable individual way, Paul Green, the most notable playwright to emerge from this aura, describes the birthpangs of dramatic creation; and George Raleigh Coffman, head of the English Department, sanely reviews the past and constructively outlines a promising course for the future. In ample detail is described by Kai Heiberg-Jurgensen the remarkable spread of popular interest in the drama fostered through extension activities; and practical plans for a dramatic art building are clearly drawn by Selden. Especial gratitude for highly competent cooperation is tendered the members of the editorial staff: Samuel Selden, for comprehensive contributions and wise criticism; Marion Fitz-Simons, for a series of vivid vignettes of the staff; Virginia Spencer, for painstaking help in making the records available.

*Chapel Hill, N. C.*  A. H.
*February 6, 1945.*

## CONTENTS

FOREWORD . . . . . . . . . . . . . . . . . . . v
FREDERICK H. KOCH—THE MAN AND HIS WORK . . . . . . 1
    Samuel Selden, *Associate Professor of Dramatic Art*
TWENTY-SIX YEARS OF THE CAROLINA PLAYMAKERS . . . . . 6
    Samuel Selden
DRAMA IN THE SOUTH . . . . . . . . . . . . . . . 7
    Frederick H. Koch, *Kenan Professor of Dramatic Art*
SCHOLIUM SCRIBENDI . . . . . . . . . . . . . . . 20
    Archibald Henderson, *Kenan Professor of Mathematics*
FIRST STAGE AND FIRST THEATRE . . . . . . . . . . . 28
    Frederick H. Koch
FROM SCRIPT TO STAGE . . . . . . . . . . . . . . 33
    Edward Muschamp, *Journalist*
DRAMATIC ART IN A UNIVERSITY PROGRAM . . . . . . . 40
    Samuel Selden
THE LYRIC LAZY SOUTH . . . . . . . . . . . . . . 50
    Paul Green, *Professor of Dramatic Art*
DRAMA IN EXTENSION . . . . . . . . . . . . . . . 54
    Kai Heiberg-Jurgensen, *Visiting Lecturer in Dramatic Art*
PRESENCE BY THE RIVER . . . . . . . . . . . . . . 63
    Paul Green
A DRAMATIC ART BUILDING . . . . . . . . . . . . . 67
    Samuel Selden
MIRACLE AT MANTEO . . . . . . . . . . . . . . . 73
    Marion Fitz-Simons, *Former Instructor in English, Woman's College of the University of North Carolina*
RETROSPECT AND PROSPECT . . . . . . . . . . . . . 75
    George R. Coffman, *Kenan Professor of English*
THE STAFF OF THE CAROLINA PLAYMAKERS . . . . . . . 78
    Marion Fitz-Simons
PLAYS PRODUCED BY THE CAROLINA PLAYMAKERS, 1918-44 . . . 87
    Virginia Page Spencer, *Assistant in Dramatic Art*
CAROLINA FOLK PLAYS PUBLISHED IN BOOKS . . . . . . . 103
    Virginia Page Spencer

# Frederick Henry Koch

*Kenan Professor of Dramatic Art, founder of The Carolina Playmakers, father of folk drama in America; teacher of Paul Green, Tom Wolfe, Jonathan Daniels, Howard Richardson, George Denny and other creative minds. Inspirer of plays expressing the lives of tenant farmers, industrial workers, Negroes, people of the mountain coves, the Piedmont, the pine barrens and the tide waters—plays of all the people. He was the champion of the democratic spirit and of the free and noble imagination. He instilled in all the eternal quest of the human spirit for a freer and better world. The man became an idea, the idea became a movement, and the movement became a national institution—the folk drama of America.*

*We shall miss him, his pipe, his dog and his jaunty step down the village streets, his constant enthusiasm as fresh as the first morning of his great hopes, now and forever a part of the life, service and traditions of the University of North Carolina. We bow our heads in sorrow and appreciation for the great loss which has come to his wife and sons, and to the University and the Nation. We lift our hearts in exceeding joy for the noble life-work of Frederick Henry Koch immortal in the plays of the people to be carried on in his name at the University of the people in the village he loved.*

*To the reverent care of all who love him we now entrust his blessed commemoration in the halls, walks and forests of Chapel Hill. He lives on in the creative spirit of youth, walking their ways, writing their plays and keeping lighted his fires from generation unto generation.*

*Frank P. Graham.*

# Frederick Henry Koch
## *The Man and His Work*

### By SAMUEL SELDEN

#### I

IN the concluding part of his commemorative tribute to Professor Frederick H. Koch on the occasion of the Twenty-First Anniversary of The Carolina Playmakers, Archibald Henderson read some verses of Vachel Lindsay's describing John Chapman, familiarly known as "Johnny Appleseed," and then remarked on the similarities between two personalities. The resemblance is striking.

The Johnny Appleseed of a century ago moved as a young man from his home in the East to the new land along the western frontier and there began a unique life work. He raised young apple trees for the pleasure and benefit of other people. Keeping ever a little in advance of civilization, he used to clear a place in the forest, plant his precious seeds, fence in the patch, and wait for the settlers to establish themselves around him. Then he would dispose of the shoots for a "fippenny bit" apiece, or give them away for nothing, and move on to prepare another nursery. Before his death he had dotted the countryside with his fruit trees.

"Johnny Appleseed" has been described as a bright-eyed, kindly, simplehearted little man who loved children, animals and all growing things; who took delight in the woods through which he walked endlessly; and who was fond of expounding to everyone who would listen to him his philosophy of goodness.

In this century, Mr. Koch reversed the pilgrimage of his prototype by moving from the West to the East. He too was a man with a kindly philosophy of human goodness who found a passionate pleasure in the beauty of the woods, in animals and flowers, but particularly in children, and in those grown people who still possess the hearts of children. He too carried with him a bag of magical seeds which he planted in many fertile places.

#### II

Frederick Henry Koch was born at Covington, Kentucky, on September 12, 1877. He was graduated from Ohio Wesleyan University in 1900,

## PIONEERING A PEOPLE'S THEATRE

and received his Master's degree from Harvard in 1909. In 1905 he accepted an appointment as instructor in English at the University of North Dakota. Here he began his long career of pioneering for an American people's theatre.

Starting at a time when any kind of scholastic theatre was generally frowned upon by university authorities, on a campus which did not boast a theatre building or even a formal stage, Frederick Koch immediately went to work to organize the interest and participation of the Dakota students. During the thirteen strenuous years he spent at that university he produced classical plays, both ancient and modern, conducted experiments in communal playwriting, and initiated the composition by students of original one-act dramas drawn from native prairie materials. He founded The Dakota Playmakers, and directed their productions of new plays both at home and on tours around the state.

When the experiments in original playmaking in the West attracted the attention of Dr. Edwin Greenlaw and Frederick Koch was persuaded through him in 1918 to come to the University of North Carolina, he extended his pioneering to the South. He organized his now famous course in playwriting, founded The Carolina Playmakers, established the Bureau of Community Drama, set up a circulating library, helped to organize a statewide Carolina Dramatic Association, and took the student plays of the Playmakers on tour to scores of big and little communities in the surrounding regions.

At the same time Professor Koch stimulated groups in various parts of North Carolina into starting experimental work in communal drama; and he lectured in all sections of the country on his favorite theme, A People's Theatre. His summer lecture and playwriting classes at Columbia, New York and Northwestern Universities and the Universities of California, Southern California, Colorado, Toledo, and Alberta and Manitoba, Canada, stirred into creative action individuals and groups far beyond the borders of the home state.

Throughout his career at North Dakota and North Carolina and in the many other centers he touched in this country and in Canada, Frederick Koch was, like the former Johnny Appleseed, a persistent planter. He took a boyish delight in each opportunity to journey to some spot where he had never been before. Always he carried with him his precious seed, and never did he return without sowing some of it. "Preaching the Gospel," he called his labors.

# FREDERICK HENRY KOCH
## III

The historian who wishes to arrive at an understanding of Professor Koch's working philosophy must recognize four motive forces which gave vitality to everything he did. The first was his dynamic faith in young people. Himself the embodiment of youth with all its enthusiastic optimism and its love of fresh adventure, he was drawn inevitably to the company of those who view life constantly with the eyes of hope. In the alert, unwearied, ever-searching faces of young people, Professor Koch saw, with never a shadow of doubt, the future of America.

The second force lay in his belief that every man alive possesses somewhere within him the creative spark, and that this needs only a little tending to be made into a flame. This faith moved through all his work with his students, especially those laboring to compose plays. More than anything he imparted to them by way of technical advice, it led them to accomplishments which were often surprising even to them. Proof to support Mr. Koch's belief in the natural talents of men and women lies in the eleven volumes of folk plays which represent the work in most part of people who had never attempted to write even short passages of dialogue before they had come into contact with their teacher. It lies also in the more mature work of such writers as Tom Wolfe, Paul Green, Jonathan Daniels, Betty Smith, Bernice Kelly Harris, Josephina Niggli, Noel Houston, and others.

The third drive in Professor Koch's work may be found in his conviction that the most dramatic things in life are usually those which may be associated with common experience. Out of this belief developed his long preoccupation with subject matter he termed "folk." Every man, he observed, is a product of his environment. Every young writer, therefore, works most successfully with materials which he sees, not afar off, out of range of his personal every-day feeling, but near at hand—those which touch him most intimately at every turn of his existence. Since nearly all young Americans are by training first regional in outlook rather than cosmopolitan, they are wise when they focus their beginning writing frankly on regional models. Out of a faithful study of individuals in their home communities the authors gradually acquire an understanding of men and women everywhere. "A knowledge of the universal," Professor Koch remarked frequently, "springs from an investigation of the specific." He had little patience with smart young dramatists who persist in trying to make plays about such glamorous but misty subjects as the court of Eighteenth Century Spain, or the super-sophisticated manners of a much-imagined but never experienced Park Avenue.

The fourth spur in Professor Koch's life was his love of the dramatic. When he was a boy, he wanted very much to be an actor. Because his eminently respectable parents were horrified at that idea, Mr. Koch became a teacher. But, although he clothed himself with the gown of academic dignity, he actually had his way; for the position he made and the organization he built around himself were designed and maintained with showmanship to the end. His life was motivated ever by a desire to shape his particular part of the world into a beautiful play—a play full of laughing young people among whom he would have his role of the grand old man with his pipe and his dog.

As a wise showman, Professor Koch saw clearly that fine plays are not made out of false-faces and tinseled gadgets, but out of simple materials viewed with love and modeled with imagination into living forms of action. And so he devoted his energy and enthusiasm to promoting "folk" subject matter. Many of the young people in his classes disagreed with him. But in the end they knew he was right. Later they told him so, and then he was happy.

## IV

As a typical pioneer, Frederick Koch was an explorer, a breaker of new ground, a planter of seed; only to a limited extent was he a husbandman. Much of the practical cultivation of the orchards he started he left to other hands. His colleagues worked out the details of academic curricula, drafted the yearly calendar of The Carolina Playmakers, managed the routine of Experimental Productions, and handled the development of Extension activities. They also served as guides and consultants in the planning of new projects. Although he was all his life a vigorous initiator of creative work, Mr. Koch was not himself primarily a creator. However, he had an enormous power. This sprang from two great gifts. First, his ability to inspire. His words were magnetic. They were compelling. No one in his presence ever went to sleep. Possessed of boundless energy, Professor Koch stirred the people about him into activity through the sheer force of his propinquity.

His second great gift was his ability to dramatize. Throughout his life he was essentially an actor, a trouper, a showman, a natural publicist. Everything he touched was interesting to him and he made it a point to see that everyone around him should know about it and be stirred up about it. In this he was eminently successful. Without Mr. Koch's talent for dramatizing and publicizing, The Carolina Playmakers and the other projects he initiated might, quite conceivably, have lapsed into plodding activities, pedestrian and conventional. He sang to his work and about it, and his song made it dance with life.

Friend and champion of youth, apostle of drama in the lives of simple men and women, actor, showman and prophet—and ever Johnny Appleseed—Frederick Henry Koch was a unique figure in the theatre and in the literary and educational world of America. His influence is already incalculable. It will doubtless increase as the years go on.

# Twenty-Six Years Of The Carolina Playmakers

| | |
|---|---|
| 1905-1918. | Professor Koch taught at University of North Dakota. Initiated work in folk-playwriting, and founded The Dakota Playmakers. |
| 1918-1919. | Professor Koch joined the faculty of Department of English at University of North Carolina. Established his now famous course, English 31, in Playwriting, and founded The Carolina Playmakers. |
| 1919 (March 14, 15). | The Playmakers produced their first bill of Original Plays. |
| 1919 (July 31). | First Forest Theatre Production. |
| 1920 (Oct. 18-20). | Professor Koch produced his pageant, *Raleigh, the Shepherd of the Ocean*, in connection with Raleigh Tercentenary Celebration, at Raleigh, North Carolina. |
| 1921 (May 7-14). | The Carolina Playmakers made their first tour. |
| 1922. | Publication of *Carolina Folk Plays, First Series*. |
| 1925 (Nov. 23). | The Playmakers Theatre, present home of The Carolina Playmakers, dedicated by President Harry Woodburn Chase. |
| 1926 (Fall). | Paul Green's play, *In Abraham's Bosom*, produced at the Provincetown Playhouse, New York. Won Pulitzer Prize. |
| 1927 (Fall). | Samuel Selden joined faculty as Instructor in English and Technical Director of The Carolina Playmakers. |
| 1928 (March). | First issue of *The Carolina Play-Book* published by The Carolina Playmakers. |
| 1928 (April 4, 5). | *Southern Regional Conference on the Drama* held in Playmakers Theatre. |
| 1933 (Feb. 3-5). | Shaw-Henderson Festival held in Playmakers Theatre. |
| 1934 (Feb.2-3). | Playmakers produced their first operetta in collaboration with the Department of Music. |
| 1934 (April 29-May 2) | Playmakers presented three plays at the first National Folk Festival in St. Louis. |
| 1936 (Spring). | Dramatic curriculum separated from English and set up in a new Department of Dramatic Art, headed by Professor Koch. A full graduate program developed. |
| 1937-1941. | Five summer productions of Paul Green's historical play with music, *The Lost Colony*, staged and directed by Samuel Selden on Roanoke Island, North Carolina. Presented by Roanoke Island Historical Association. |
| 1939 (April 1-6). | *Drama in the South* conference held in Playmakers Theatre. |
| 1939 (Fall). | Initiation of work in Radio Production under Earl Wynn. |
| 1939-1940. | Two fall productions of Paul Green's Scottish Historical Drama, *The Highland Call*, directed by John W. Parker for the Cape Fear Valley Scottish Festival at Fayetteville, North Carolina. |
| 1941 (Oct.-Dec.) | Tour of the Repertory Company of The Carolina Playmakers, presenting Paul Green's *The House of Connelly*, directed by Samuel Selden and managed by Harry Davis. |
| 1943 (May 19). | The remodeled Forest Theatre dedicated by President Frank Porter Graham. |
| 1943 (Dec. 10). | Professor Koch gave, in Memorial Hall, his 39th annual reading of Dickens' *A Christmas Carol*. |
| 1944 (Aug. 16). | Professor Koch died at Miami Beach, Florida. |
| 1944 (Dec. 12). | The Playmakers presented the 100th performance in their Experimental Series of New Plays. |

# Drama In The South

### By FREDERICK H. KOCH

TODAY The Playmakers of Carolina welcome you to our home town of Chapel Hill, to our historic little theatre building, the first state owned theatre in America to be dedicated to the making of its own native drama. We are thinking today of the simple beginnings of The Carolina Playmakers on the improvised stage in our village high school auditorium twenty-one years ago. And the little homespun plays that found an eager and lusty response. Before this, Barrett Clark avers that North Carolina was regarded by Samuel French, leading publisher of plays in the United States and England, as a "dead" state—so lacking in dramatic interest that the entire state had been stricken from their mailing list as not being worth the price of postage to carry their catalogues! The immediate success of the first little CAROLINA FOLK PLAYS suggested to us here the hope for a possible oasis in the South, dubbed by H. L. Mencken then, "The Sahara of the Bozart."

### DAKOTA FOLK PLAYS

And in thinking of our adventure in native playwriting in Chapel Hill, now coming of age, we remember too the twelve years of pioneer experiment at the frontier University of North Dakota before that time—when the Little Theatre movement was still to come. Maxwell Anderson, now distinguished American playwright, was one of the founders of our first dramatic society there and out of the group of which he was a charter member came The Dakota Playmakers and the first PRAIRIE FOLK PLAYS. On receiving a playbill of the first original Dakota plays young Anderson wrote from California, where he was then engaged in teaching: "If there is anything that would bring me back to the old sod, it is a dramatic revival; and honestly, it seems to me that if the interest and enthusiasm keep up we may yet have one comparable to the recent flowering in Ireland. I would be willing to walk all the way back to the Dakota prairie to get in on that." And when later he went to New York the first play he wrote, you remember, was *White*

---

❡ An address delivered by Frederick H. Koch in The Playmakers Theatre at Chapel Hill, North Carolina, on April 5, 1940, for the Southern Regional Theatre Festival commemorating the founding of The Carolina Playmakers in 1918-19.

## PIONEERING A PEOPLE'S THEATRE

*Desert,* a play of the vast winter plain of Dakota—its loneliness—a native play of the prairie. He had made a beginning.

The plays of Dakota were often crude, but they were honest. Simple folk plays, near to the good, strong, wind-swept soil—plays telling of long, bitter winters in the little sod shanty. But plays singing, too, of the prairie springtime, of unflected sunshine, of the wilderness gay with wild roses, of the fenceless fields welling over with lark song. Plays of the travail and achievement of a pioneer people!

### THE BEGINNINGS IN CAROLINA

The only male member of the first playwriting course at Chapel Hill in the fall of 1918 was Thomas Wolfe, "Tom" to us, a lanky six-and-a-half-foot tall mountain lad with burning eyes. The other twelve members of the class were co-eds. After the meeting of the class that first day he said, by way of apology, "'Proff', I don't want you to think that this Ladies Aid Society represents Carolina. We have a lot of he-men seriously interested in writing here, but they are all disguised in army uniforms now. I tried to get into one myself but they didn't have one long enough for me."

His first play—and his first published work—*The Return of Buck Gavin,* a tragedy of a mountain outlaw, included in the second volume of CAROLINA FOLK PLAYS, was one of the plays in our initial production that first season. We couldn't find anyone to play the part and I said to him, "I guess you'll have to play it yourself, Tom. You may not know it, but you really wrote that part for yourself!"

"But I can't act, 'Proff,' I've never acted."

"You're a born actor," I assured him, "and you *are* Buck Gavin."

I shall never forget his first performance. With free mountain stride, his dark eyes blazing, he became the hunted outlaw of the Great Smokies. There was something uncanny in his acting of the part—something of the pent-up fury of his highland forbears.

In his foreword to *The Return of Buck Gavin* Tom wrote for all beginners: "It is the fallacy of the young writer to picture the dramatic as unusual and remote.... The dramatic is not unusual. It is happening daily in our lives."

Of his playwriting that first year he wrote: "I have written about people I have known and concerning whom I feel qualified to write. They have suggested a train of thought that intensely interests me, and is, I believe, of vital importance to me. My writing, I feel sure, has been made easier and better by their production.

## DRAMA IN THE SOUTH

"If they have affected my writing to this extent—if they have indirectly caused an analysis of my work, and a determination of my future course—are they not worthwhile, even though they be but the amateurish productions of a youngster?"

It is interesting to recall now the first efforts of the young writer. Like Anderson, he wrote what he knew. Though crude, those who have followed him through the years cannot fail to see in his first hastily written little plays the indications of his later achievement in *Look Homeward, Angel* and *Of Time and the River*.

### THE CAROLINA FOLK PLAYS

As far as we have been able to determine, the first use of the term "folk play" in the American theatre was The Carolina Playmakers' announcement: CAROLINA FOLK PLAYS on the playbill of their initial production in Chapel Hill twenty-one years ago. The first play presented was *When Witches Ride*, about folk superstition in Northampton county, by Elizabeth Lay of Beaufort, North Carolina (now Mrs. Paul Green), which we are reviving with the original cast on Saturday evening. Now the term is not unfamiliar in the expanding scene of our American theatre. Witness Paul Green's *In Abraham's Bosom*, Lulu Vollmer's *Sun-Up*, Dorothy and DuBose Heyward's *Porgy*, Jack Kirkland's dramatization of Erskine Caldwell's *Tobacco Road*, Lynn Riggs' *Green Grow the Lilacs*, Thornton Wilder's *Our Town* and Robert Sherwood's *Abe Lincoln in Illinois*.

From the first our particular interest in North Carolina has been the use of native materials and the making of fresh dramatic forms. We have found that if the writer observes the locality with which he is most familiar and interprets it faithfully, it may show him the way to the universal. If he can see the interestingness of the lives of those about him with understanding and imagination, with wonder, why may he not interpret that life in significant images for others—perhaps for all? It has been so in all lasting art.

Four volumes of CAROLINA FOLK PLAYS by different authors and a volume of Paul Green's early plays, also written in the playwriting courses at the University of North Carolina over a period of years, have been published and widely produced in the United States and abroad. The materials were drawn by each writer from scenes familiar and near, often from remembered adventures of his youth, from folk tales and the common tradition, and from present-day life in North Carolina. They are plays of native expressiveness, of considerable range and variety, presenting scenes from the remote coves of the Great Smoky Mountains to the dangerous shoals of Cape Hatteras.

Our recent volume, AMERICAN FOLK PLAYS, marks the extension of our North Carolina idea of folk playmaking to other American states, to Canada and to Mexico. It represents the work of twenty new playwrights, eighteen from the United States—all the way from California and the Rocky Mountain regions to Florida and New England—and one from Western Canada, and one from beyond the Rio Grande in Mexico. The plays included were selected from hundreds of scripts written and produced by students in playwriting at Chapel Hill and in summer courses it has been my privilege to conduct in some of our leading universities: Columbia, New York, Northwestern, Colorado, California (both Berkeley and Los Angeles), Southern California, and Alberta, Canada.

In writing of this anthology (in *The Saturday Review of Literature* of July 1, 1939) under the caption, "The Native Theatre," Stephen Vincent Benet notes: "Each Playmaker has honestly tried to get to grips with some one aspect of American life. It may be Davy Crockett or a farm woman of the North Dakota prairies—it may be a cowboy comedy or an Oklahoma tragedy—the same desire to work with native materials and make something of them is obvious in them all. It is an interesting and, in many respects, a remarkable achievement." And the English reviewer of the *Literary Supplement* of *The London Times* wrote on September 9, 1939: "Those who are tired of thrillers, drawing-room comedies and film fantasies will find these tragedies, farces, and sketches from real life refreshing. . . . It would be worthwhile seeing whether similar 'folk' plays could not still be evoked from our English scene and so bring to the drama a fertilizing influence."

## Folk Drama Defined

The term "folk," as we use it, has nothing to do with the folk play of medieval times. But rather is it concerned with folk subject matter: with the legends, superstitions, customs, environmental differences, and the vernacular of the common people. For the most part they are realistic and human; sometimes they are imaginative and poetic.

The chief concern of the folk dramatist is man's conflict with the forces of nature and his simple pleasure in being alive. The conflict may not be apparent on the surface in the immediate action on the stage. But the ultimate cause of all dramatic action we classify as "folk," whether it be physical or spiritual, may be found in man's desperate struggle for existence and

## DRAMA IN THE SOUTH

in his enjoyment of the world of nature. The term "folk" with us applies to that form of drama which is earth-rooted in the life of our common humanity.

For many years our playwrights of the South—indeed of all America—were imitative, content with reproducing the outlived formulas of the old world. There was nothing really *native* about them. Whenever they did write of American life, the treatment was superficial and innocuous.

### THE NEGRO DRAMA

When Augustus Thomas wrote *Alabama* and *In Mizzoura* optimistic heralds announced the arrival of the "great American drama"; but the playwright barely skimmed the surfaces of these colorful states. His next play, *The Witching Hour,* had something of the jessamine perfume of Kentucky romance, but the ghost of the old well-made melodrama was lugged in to resolve the plot. Then there was *Uncle Tom's Cabin,* a grand old theatre piece, but its treatment of the southern Negro, though sincere, was sentimental. Four native North Carolinians have contributed authentic drama of the Southern scene to the contemporary theatre: Paul Green, a challenging tragedy of the Negro race *In Abraham's Bosom,* Lulu Vollmer and Hatcher Hughes, dramas of the mountain people, *Sun-Up* and *Hell Bent for Heaven,* and Ann Preston Bridgers, domestic tragedy in a small-town, *Coquette.* Following Paul Green came Dorothy and DuBose Heyward with *Porgy,* of a Negro neighborhood in Charleston; and Roark Bradford's stories of the *Green Pastures* from Louisiana, to go singing along for five years all over America. And this week Randolph Edmonds, talented Negro playwright, brings to our Festival stage a tragedy of his own people, *Breeders,* to be enacted by a group of Negro players from Dillard University in New Orleans. The Negro theatre has come a long way in twenty-one years. I recall Paul Green's first Negro play written for the playwriting group at Chapel Hill, *White Dresses,* of a lovely Mulatto girl, Mary McLean—"a tragedy in black and white," he calls it.

Paul said, "I have written that part for you, Elizabeth," referring to Elizabeth Taylor who later played important roles in Brock Pemberton's productions on Broadway for five years.

"I would love to do it!"

But the time was not ripe, although North Carolina was a leader among the Southern states in Negro education and in friendly race relationships. We had to wait. It was with great satisfaction in later years that this same play was brought to our Playmakers' stage by a visiting group of Negro players from St. Augustine's College in Raleigh. And now we have flourishing Negro inter-collegiate and inter-high school dramatic tournaments each spring in North Carolina. The Jim Crow sentiment of the old South is gone and an audience crowded our big Memorial Hall to the rafters when Richard B. Harrison, formerly a teacher in Greensboro, North Carolina, came to Chapel Hill with *The Green Pastures.*

### TENANT FARM DRAMA

Twenty-one years ago Harold Williamson, a student in the playwriting class from nearby Carthage, brought to our makeshift stage in the high school the first play of the Southern sharecropper—hitherto undiscovered by the American theatre as far as is known. It was a little tragedy about a tenant farm girl, *Peggy.* The drab cabin that was her home which we had passed a thousand times as a dull sight, on the stage became suddenly something new, something interesting, something wonderful. Here the jaded farm woman, Mag, with snuffstick protruding from the corner of her mouth, getting supper of corn bread and fat back, singing the while snatches of an old ballad, was no longer a commonplace figure. She had been transformed by the magic of the theatre. The tragic fact of her hard-won existence had become a reality to us—life itself that moves and feels—a gripping drama! A neglected chapter of the Southern scene had come to life on our stage.

A little later came Paul and Erma Green's little drama of the grinding poverty of the sharecropper's life in *Fixin's* in which the pent fury of the work-driven wife, Lilly Robinson, is portrayed with grim and terrible reality. She craves a little beauty, "purty fixin's." But her husband's eyes cannot see beyond the sod he plows. The scene is a bare cabin home in Harnett County, North Carolina, but the theme is universal—the pitiful conflict of two natures which are irreconcilable.

The next morning after our Playmakers' tour performance of *Fixin's* in Atlanta, before a sophisticated audience in evening dress, a man came to me and said, "I think I owe it to you to tell you of the effect that little play, *Fixin's,* had on me last night.—I come from New York, and I've been seeing the best shows in the theatre there for thirty years. But that little play last night *got* me so much that, before I went to bed, I went to the Western Union office and telegraphed some flowers to my wife in New York!"

And after a performance in western North Carolina, the reviewer in the *Greensboro Daily News* wrote: "*Fixin's* presented a scene of such stark and terrible reality as to make at least one person in the audience want to rise up and say, 'This thing has got to be stopped.' " The little play had gone beyond the theatre into life itself.

Today the plight of this forgotten class of country people has been vividly portrayed—for better or for worse—in Jack Kirkland's sensational treatment of Erskine Caldwell's story of the degenerate poor white sharecropper of the backlands of Georgia in *Tobacco Road*. And the tragi-comic figure of an irrepressible Jeeter Lester has held the stage for more than five seasons now.

## Trouping

From the first The Carolina Playmakers have been interested in the making of a native theatre throughout the state and beyond their own borders. Traveling in their Show-Bus, with three sets of homemade scenery atop, portable lighting equipment, costumes, and stage properties, they have played all over North Carolina, in cross-roads villages in the mountains and in "neighborhoods" by the sea — in school auditoriums, old-time opera houses, and outlived town halls.

The Playmakers' present trouping facilities offer a striking contrast to the first tour of The Dakota Playmakers over 800 miles of treeless plains when it was necessary to spend several hours at a junction point sometimes waiting for an "accommodation" train to take them to a little prairie town at the end of a branch line. Then the players drew lots to see who would peddle the handbills to advertise their arrival in town. Now The Playmakers ride in royal fashion over the hills and through the valleys of the Blue Ridge, blossoming with dogwood and flaming with the judas trees of a Carolina spring; now announced in three-sheet posters in gay colors, and by high praise in the newspapers, their coming is like a triumphal entry.

The thirty-six tours of The Playmakers have not been confined to North Carolina. We have played in one hundred and twenty-one different towns and cities—all the way from south Georgia to Boston, Massachusetts, and as far west as the National Folk Festivals at St. Louis and at Dallas, Texas, playing three hundred and twenty-two performances to a total audience of more than three hundred thousand. In their thirty-six tours The Carolina Playmakers have played forty-five of the folk plays written and produced originally at Chapel Hill. They have played in the beautiful University Theatre at Yale, on three successive tours at Columbia University in New York City, and twice at the Fine Arts Theatre in Boston, where the troupe

## PIONEERING A PEOPLE'S THEATRE

was greeted by Governor Frank Allen at the Massachusetts State House. On our first visit to Washington, D. C., we were cordially received at the White House by President Calvin Coolidge, who actually went so far as to say he thought our work was "very interesting."

Of The Playmakers' first appearance in New York the reviewer of the *Theatre Magazine* wrote: "The rare characters and the homely qualities of these plays linger in one's memory long after some of the more sophisticated plays of Broadway have been forgotten. In fact, each time we witness a program of the Carolina Folk Plays, we feel for the moment that we, too, are just 'folks'—along with those other folks on the other side of the footlights, who transport us for a brief but happy period back to their hill country, with its rich traditions, legends, and folklore."

### Drama in Extension

Simultaneous with the organization of The Carolina Playmakers at the University twenty-one years ago was that of the Bureau of Community Drama as a unit of the Extension Division. At first the work was conducted by correspondence and by a play-lending and bulletin service. Later the demand was such that a traveling Field Director was provided to assist schools and rural communities in the writing and production of plays, pageants, and festivals. In 1925 the state-wide Carolina Dramatic Association was formed which, under the aegis of John W. Parker of our Department of Dramatic Art, is holding its Seventeenth Annual Festival and State Tournament here this week as a part of the anniversary celebration. The membership of the Association now includes one hundred and one college, high school, and country theatres from all parts of North Carolina from the Great Smoky Mountains to the shoals of Hatteras.

A remarkable development of the North Carolina state organization is the annual National Folk Festival now held in this, the seventh year, in Washington, D. C. The founder of the National Folk Festival, Sarah Gertrude Knott, resigned as State Representative of the Bureau of Community Drama in North Carolina to become the founder and director of the nation-wide celebration of American folk arts. "If one state, North Carolina, can do it," Miss Knott asked, "why not the United States?" She has succeeded beyond all expectations.

### Plays of a Country Neighborhood

In this connection it is interesting to note the achievement of Bernice Kelly Harris, author of *Purslane* and of a recent volume of Folk Plays of Eastern

## DRAMA IN THE SOUTH

CAROLINA, of her own country neighborhood in Northampton County, North Carolina, not far from the Roanoke River. These plays of the simple lives and homely ways of her neighbors and friends were produced originally in her home town of Seaboard and brought in successive years to the annual festivals of the Carolina Dramatic Association at Chapel Hill. Bernice Harris, as a teacher of English in a rural high school, was a member of the first summer playwriting group in Chapel Hill twenty-one years ago. She was so captivated by her first adventure in playwriting that she was impelled to pass on to her boys and girls the new wonder she had found in folk playmaking. "I saw the beauty of a new sort of humanism," she has written of that first summer.

### MEXICAN FOLK PLAYS

Since publishing five volumes of Carolina plays and a book of twenty American folk plays, The Playmakers issued in 1938 a volume of MEXICAN FOLK PLAYS written at Chapel Hill by Josephina Niggli of Monterrey, Nuevo Leon, Mexico, and produced originally in The Playmakers Theatre here. Plays of the humble lives of her own people, their restless history, their legends and the childlike wonder of their folkways. These Mexican plays have been widely produced throughout the United States and Canada, and many times abroad.

### CAROLINA AND CANADA

Sometimes our home-grown plays of Chapel Hill are transplanted to far places. A play of the Canadian frontier, *Still Stands the House*, which Gwendolyn Pharis of Magrath, Alberta, Canada, wrote here in 1938, was last year awarded the first prize of $100, as the best native Canadian play entered in the annual Dominion Drama Festival in 1939.

Another case. *Funeral Flowers for the Bride*, written for The Playmakers in 1937 by Beverley DuBose Hamer of Eastover, South Carolina (who vowed at the first that she "couldn't write a play") won first place in England in the International One Act Play Competition of 1938 over one hundred and sixty-six plays entered. It was produced in London at the Duchess Theatre on November 27 of that year.

### A CHINESE PLAYMAKER

A Chinese boy came to Chapel Hill for playwriting: Cheng-Chin Hsiung of Nanchang, China.

"Hsiung," I inquired, "what kind of play do you want to write?"

## PIONEERING A PEOPLE'S THEATRE

"I want to write a play about the Chinese-American problem—a mixed marriage of a Chinese boy and an American girl."

"A good idea, but you can't do it.—We should like to have you write of your own people. You have a marvelous store of legend in old China. We are interested here in what we call the 'folk play.' I wish you would write for us a Chinese folk play."

"If you let me write this Chinese-American marriage play first, then I will write for you a Chinese folk play."

"Hsiung," I said, "you know that you can't understand the mind of an American girl."

"Well, I have been in this country five years."

"Five years! Some of us have lived here fifty years, and we cannot do it! But go ahead, write your problem play first; then write a real Chinese play." So he wrote a play called *Poor Polly*—and it was well named!

Then he went to the storehouse of old China and wrote a charming play, *The Thrice Promised Bride*, in the manner of the Chinese stage—a play of romance, of comedy, of poetry. We were so much impressed with it that I sent it to the editor of *Theatre Arts*, who wrote back, "I like it so much that I want to publish it in our next issue." There Frank Shay saw it and wrote for permission to include it in his anthology *Twenty-Five Short Plays, International*, as the only play in the volume representing China. There Henry Lanier, editor of the *Golden Book*, saw it and paid $105.00 for permission to reprint it.

So *Poor Polly* passed and *The Thrice Promised Bride* arrived. Then he wrote another Chinese play, *The Marvelous Romance of Wen Chun-Chin*, which was published in *Poet Lore*.

Our Chinese Playmaker's plays have been favorites not only in the United States but especially in England; and we sent him a royalty check for a performance not long ago in far away Kuala Lumpur, Straits Settlements.

### THE CAROLINA PLAY-BOOK

Besides publishing plays The Playmakers have issued twelve volumes of a unique little quarterly, THE CAROLINA PLAY-BOOK, devoted to the making of a native theatre. THE PLAY-BOOK has the distinction of being included for two seasons in the International Exhibit of Periodicals at the Century of Progress Exposition in Chicago as one of only three American theatre journals—the other two being *Theatre Arts* and *Stage*. A valuable supplement to THE PLAY-BOOK is THE CAROLINA STAGE, an attractive publication in mimeographed form, designed to meet the practical needs of the members of the Carolina Dramatic Association.

### The Professional and the People's Theatre

From the first The Carolina Playmakers have been interested primarily in the making of a people's theatre, and a host of our graduates have gone back to their home towns and cities near and far resolved to do their bit in the making of such a theatre in America. Of course a number of Playmakers have escaped to the professional theatre and found success there; more recently, Shepperd Strudwick and Eugenia Rawls on Broadway and Lionel Stander and Kay Kyser in Hollywood. Although successful on the New York stage in his early days, George Denny found a wider field for his talents. Now he is President of New York's Town Hall and director of the NBC "Town Hall of the Air," which he founded.

Shepperd Strudwick (from the village of Hillsboro, just twelve miles from Chapel Hill), after several years of struggle on Broadway, found a place in the New York Theatre Guild. More recently he has been the leading spirit in a group of young actors, The Surry Players. He has had considerable success with M-G-M in the pictures too. Only last week I received an enthusiastic letter from him in Hollywood. "The more experience I have in the theatre," he writes, "the more strongly do I yearn for the theatre of Paul Green's *Johnny Johnson* and *The Lost Colony,* plays that excite me more than anything the theatre has had to offer for years. *Abe Lincoln in Illinois* and *The Grapes of Wrath* do it in the movies and I hope to get a shot at it here before I get through.... The times are ripe now to receive what The Playmakers have to give with a more open understanding than ever before. The times need The Playmakers badly now. That's why *The Lost Colony* project is so exciting to me."

### Communal Drama of American History

Paul Green's *The Lost Colony*, you recall, was written and produced originally in the summer of 1937 to commemorate the 350th anniversary of the first English settlement in America. It has played for three seasons now on Roanoke Island to tens of thousands of people in an outdoor theatre on the actual site of the landing of our first English colonists. Brooks Atkinson in an article in *The New York Times* not long ago, "Ought We to Found a National Theatre?", is eternally right in saying that *The Lost Colony* has become a permanent part of the culture of the people on Roanoke Island. He goes on, "As long as they live, these people will have a grander notion of our heritage than they had before this reverent drama was written."

## PIONEERING A PEOPLE'S THEATRE

In November of the present year Mr. Green wrote a second drama for the American people's theatre, *The Highland Call*, commemorating the bicentennial of Scotch settlement in the Cape Fear River valley of southeastern North Carolina, the stirring events of Revolutionary times and the heroic leadership of bonnie Flora Macdonald. Extending the idea of communal playmaking in *The Lost Colony*, *The Highland Call* was produced in Fayetteville by The Carolina Playmakers in collaboration with the citizens of that historic town. It evoked such enthusiasm there that plans have been completed for its annual production.

Now Mr. Green is at work on the third drama of his trilogy of early American history. It is to be given for the first time in old Williamsburg, Virginia, beginning early in June and closing before the opening of the summer-long run of *The Lost Colony* on Roanoke Island. Mr. Green holds that America was regarded by the under-privileged classes in the old world as a "land of opportunity," and that this was the compelling motive and promise which brought all classes to our shores and which America must fulfill to validate her beginnings.

Brooks Atkinson observes further in the above-mentioned article that we are just coming to realize that our country is rich in folklore and "should yield an abundant harvest of drama, and a national theatre that will serve the entire country, should develop regional plays and contribute to a deeper national understanding." I know of no better way toward an imaginative, a spiritual expression of our tradition of democracy.

### Coming of Age

From the first we have thought of our Playmakers as a fellowship of young people working happily together toward a single ideal—the making of a communal, a people's theatre in America. Walt Whitman happily expresses it, "An institution of the dear love of comrades." Important as the individual is in the theatre, it is well for us to remind ourselves constantly that the dramatic is essentially a social art. Whatever The Playmakers have achieved is due primarily to their holding fast together to such an objective. Whatever we have done, we have done together.

We have come a long way in twenty-one years. Beginning traditionally in the Department of English as a one-man theatre we now have a separate Department of Dramatic Art with a full-time theatre staff; and, in lieu of the traditional research thesis in English for the Master of Arts degree, a student may submit an original play.

A year ago the Department entered the field of cinema and radio. Films

## DRAMA IN THE SOUTH

from the Museum of Modern Art library are shown regularly in The Playmakers Theatre, and old favorites from The Playmakers' repertory (and new scripts, too) are now being broadcast from the University radio studio over a network of the Mutual Broadcasting System every Saturday afternoon at 3:30. The production this week is the first "Carolina Folk Play" of twenty-one years ago, *When Witches Ride*, by Elizabeth Lay (now Mrs. Paul Green).

Now we are wondering how long it will be before we take on television!

### Those Who Come After

Time alone can tell what will be the effect, for good or bad, of our folk playmaking. According to the editor of *Holland's, The Magazine of the South*, the influence of The Carolina Playmakers "has spread indubitably into the associated fields of the novel, the short story, and even nonfiction works. From the basic idea underlying their work and philosophy stem such writings as those of Caldwell, Heyward, Miller, Bradford, Faulkner, Stribling, and other and younger novelists. Not that many more influences have not impinged sharply and deeply on Southern writers and on Southern thought generally; but The Carolina Playmakers and their example have been a centralizing, crystallizing, and vitalizing force unequaled in Southern literature to date."

From the first we have believed in the South, we have held that the South had something rich and strange to contribute to America, something of native honesty and of beauty. Dr. Albert Shaw in writing of the beginnings in Dakota and in Carolina interpreted our hope in an editorial article in *The American Review of Reviews* of September 1919: "When every community has its own native group of plays and producers, we shall have a national American Theatre that will give a richly varied, authentic expression of American life. We shall be aware—which we are only dimly at present—of the actual pulse of the people by the expression in folk plays of their coördinated minds. It is this common vision, this collective striving that determines nationalism, and remains throughout the ages, the one and only touchstone of the future."

In thinking of the next twenty-one years I go back to a conversation of my high school days with one of Walt Whitman's friends. On his last visit to the Singer of America he remembered Old Walt standing in the door of his little home in Camden and calling out in farewell, "Expecting the main things from those who come after."

# Scholium Scribendi

## By Archibald Henderson

### I

WE live in an age of calculated advance: projected undertakings for the improvement of the present and for enhanced benefit and prosperity in the future. Post-war planning is the *mot d'ordre* of the hour. No state or institution is deemed up-to-date or progressive which does not outline constructive plans for the coming day—five year plans, ten year plans, and the like, and attempt to implement them constructively. The blue-printer is the potential educator, statesman, and leader of the future.

After twenty-six years of steady advance, under the leadership of the late Frederick H. Koch and a corps of able colleagues, The Carolina Playmakers face the future, under new leadership, and confronted by many thorny and complex problems. At this moment of transition, careful inventory and realistic assessment of tangible assets are clearly indicated as both desirable and imperative. It is not necessary to retrogress in order the better to progress— *reculer pour mieux sauter*, as the French have it. The imperative need is to balance losses and gains, and to assess the basic values and calculable gains upon which to build a more stable and beautiful structure. Such a structure, to withstand the pressure of competition and effect some adjustment to changing conditions, must be supported in part by idealism and dream; but in order to survive, this fabric of idealistic dream must be firmly woven upon the loom of the real.

### II

The Carolina Playmakers is an educational organization primarily devoted to giving instruction in the arts of the drama and the theater, with its contemporary adjuncts of the film and the radio. It is an educational organization for enhancing the qualities and values of cultural phenomena which are themselves educational in character. It is buttressed upon two extraordinary postulates: that anyone can write a play, and that everyone should write a play. These postulates, based upon faith in a certain human modicum of esthetic talent and creative power, are, like all postulates, incapable of philosophic and critical demonstration. They can only be judged in terms of their consequences; and it is the consequences of twenty-six years of "playmaking" upon which attention should be focused.

One may concede, at the outset, that any person of normal intelligence, by sufficiently prolonged and intensive study of the history and technic of the drama and the arts of the theatre, may acquire under careful supervision and meticulous instruction a certain facility in casting story in dramatic form. The many scores of plays written by Carolina Playmakers and produced with moderate and in some cases more than moderate success appear, on preliminary consideration, to validate the soundness of the postulates mentioned above. But it does not follow that the authors of these plays are playwrights in the professional sense or will succeed in the grilling competition along the "Great White Ways" of the world.

Indeed, we shall find, on reference to capable practitioners and eminent critics of the arts of drama and the theatre, that to the two postulates mentioned above must be added a third: no candidate need apply who has not a natural aptitude, an instinctive capacity, for casting story in dramatic form. This postulate has been firmly supported by two conspicuous examples of successful practicing playwright and dramatic critic respectively: Bernard Shaw and Brander Matthews. In a measure, this third requirement is met in the case of would-be playmakers, both here and in similar schools of playwriting elsewhere; and the number of candidates who fall by the wayside is surprisingly small. It is also noteworthy that, of those plays written by students and produced by The Carolina Playmakers, an appreciable number are found to be worthy of unsubsidized publication in collections of plays issued by reputable publishing firms. The eleven volumes of plays, published under the directorship of Dr. Koch, while containing a certain amount of duplication, constitute not unimpressive testimony to the success of this idealistic and pragmatic experiment in pedagogy.

The school for playwrights at Chapel Hill, it should be realized, is not *primarily* designed to provide specific preparation and immediate training for "Broadway." With the large number of original plays constantly pressing for production, time does not permit of that slick finish and streamlined perfection indispensable to metropolitan production. But for ambitious and aspiring youth there are always, agleam on the horizon, the glamour and allure of the great prizes of the drama and the theatre. There are always room and encouragement for talent and genius—although it is well recognized that the Paul Greens and the Tom Wolfes are few and far between. Yet there is always, among The Carolina Playmakers, an electric thrill—in the expectation of the arrival of a new star—whether dramatist, novelist, poet, actor, dancer, or stage director. There is always the feeling, to use Arnold's phrase, that the future of the theatre is immense.

The avowed purposes of the school are cultural study and dramatic reflection, through stage representation, of certain restricted segments of American society, the manners, customs, folkways, traditions, peculiarities of speech, dialects and all other manifestations of strata of population living close to the soil. Plays of this character, dealing "with the legends, superstitions, customs, environmental differences, and the vernacular of the common people," to quote Koch's own words, are called "folk-plays"; and the term "folk" is said to apply to "that form of drama which is earth-rooted in the life of our common humanity." The term has taken on historic significance, in that, in this specialized connotation, it is believed to have been first used in the American theatre on the playbill of the initial production of plays by The Carolina Playmakers at Chapel Hill in 1919. This form of art is distinctively novel and authentically American—a wide *démarche* from the classical meaning of folk literature, as works of communal inspiration and gradual popular evolution. The Punch and Judy show, the traditional English folk-play of "St. George and the Dragon," for examples, stand at one end of the scale; the mystery and miracle plays of the Middle Ages suffice to serve as mean; and the mighty narrative of Homer's "Iliad," with its almost infinite richness of human interest stories for dramatic representation, marks the apex of popular story, whether history, legend, tradition, or sheer invention, slowly filtered down through the sieve of native record and communal transmission.

### III

In looking towards the future policy of The Carolina Playmakers, the question of enlargement of the scope and widening of the aims of the organization naturally arises. The comparatively brief period of apprenticeship here argues conclusively that, as at present constituted, the organization cannot aspire, even if this were its aim, to serve as a school of direct training for "Broadway." There be some who regard Thomas Wolfe as a gifted playwright "lost" to the American theatre, although he engaged in intensive preparation for the profession of playwriting for some six years. Walter Prichard Eaton has expressed the firm conviction that at least ten years of academic and theater study are indispensable as a preliminary to Broadway competition.

The enlargement of the scope and aims of The Carolina Playmakers, it would appear, does not lie in the direction of specific training for Broadway. New vistas, however, open in other directions. The domination of the folk-play idea, useful as this has been because of a natural and untapped reservoir of material ready to hand, cannot continue indefinitely. A point of saturation for any soil is ultimately reached; and the necessity arises for the exploitation of new and virgin areas. The "naïve wonder" which made the early Carolina folk play so effective has lost much of its poignancy for the more sophisticated drama students and would-be playwrights of Chapel Hill. Student dramatic authors of the future, as pointed out by William Peery in his essay on *Carolina Playmaking*, which won the Gray Essay Award of the Dramatists' Alliance at Stanford University in 1939, "will have to face problems typical of today or lose that creative power of native materials which largely accounts for the success of folk movements in the past."

Surely the lesson to be learned and the moral to be drawn are clear. Subject matter however quaint; vernacular however autochthonous; myth, legend, or tradition, however bizarre, cannot take the place of authentic dramatic inspiration; nor can stories bearing these features dispense with esthetic forms of interpretation and universalization. "To hold, as 'twere, the mirror up to nature," as a means of reflecting the eccentricities, whimsicalities, and bizarreries of peculiar and isolated segments of population, usually remote from civilization's contagion and culture's impact, is not enough— even on the authority of so supreme a dramatist as Shakespeare. It is necessary to sift out, from the heterogeneous stream of sentient life, the significant features of human experience; and to give those features, in dramatic form, the sequential collocation of self-interpretation, and to impart to them the enduring investiture of art.

## IV

In focusing attention upon local folk-materials and revealing to other sections the particular features of North Carolina character and the Southeastern *milieu*, The Carolina Playmakers have rendered yeoman service in the pioneer period of their activities. From the social, industrial, sociological, and religious viewpoints, it is highly important that the conditions under which various underprivileged classes live and suffer and survive should be brought to light. The South, as regarded by a liberal President, is economic problem Number 1; and various remedial measures have been proposed and some even put into effect. But it is one thing to regard the South as an economic ward of the Nation, and quite another to proceed upon the assumption that the only materials suitable for dramatic treatment which the South affords are the share-croppers, the "crackers," the mud-eaters, the pallid victims of the hookworm, the tenant farmers, the underpaid and exploited millworkers, the Negro.

The drama is a universal, not a particularistic, art. It takes all humanity in its scope. In any effort towards advance, full recognition should be taken of this universal quality of dramatic literature and of the drama as theatric representation. A clearer picture of the people and a wider perspective of the entire region will be obtained if all phases of life be taken into dramatic survey. North Carolina history is rich to overflowing in materials well adapted to dramatic treatment. The novels of Inglis Fletcher, for example, clearly point the way in this direction: the treatment for literary purposes of historical materials of vivid human interest and romantic appeal. Paul Green's "The Lost Colony" affords a conspicuous example of the pageant-drama quarried out of historic materials. The thrilling stories of the early colonists, the wanderings of the Palatines, the contributions of the Moravians, the Scotch-Covenanters, and the Huguenot refugees, the pioneering of Daniel Boone and his companions, the founding of Boonesborough and Nashville, the opening of the West, the careers of William R. Davie, Andrew Jackson, Thomas Hart Benton, Andrew Johnson, James K. Polk, Nathaniel Rochester, Sam Houston, John Sevier, James Robertson, Hinton Rowan Helper, and Benjamin Sherwood Hedrick; the glories and the tragedies of the brothers' war, the horrors of "Reconstruction" and the grim, dark endeavors of the Ku Klux Klan—these are topics which, from among countless others, come readily to mind.

In this proposal of a broader treatment of regional themes and individual, political, and social problems, of all classes of the population and all strata of society, there is no suggestion that, in preoccupation with the universal, the dramas of the future to be written here should ignore or neglect the distinguishing *mores* and characteristic qualities, speech, and *Weltanschauung* of the people of this region. Koch always rightly laid stress upon writing about "the life and the people we live with and know—here and now." And the injunction has never been better expressed than by Bernard Shaw:

"The writer who aims at producing the platitudes which are 'not for an age, but for all time' has his reward in being unreadable in all ages; whilst

## SCHOLIUM SCRIBENDI

Plato and Aristophanes trying to knock some sense into the Athens of their day, Shakespeare peopling that same Athens with Elizabethan mechanics and Warwickshire hunts, Ibsen photographing the local doctors and vestrymen of a Norwegian parish, Carpaccio painting the life of St. Ursula exactly as if she were a lady living in the next street to him, are still alive and at home everywhere among the dust and ashes of many thousands of academic, punctilious, most archaeologically correct men of letters who spend their lives haughtily avoiding the journalist's vulgar obsession with the ephemeral."

V

The average person, even if he or she has attended performances by The Carolina Playmakers, scarcely realizes the extent and range of the instruction. The popular impression is that pupils are taught merely how to act and how to write one-act plays. Actually the instruction covers Shakespeare, American drama, modern drama, comparative drama, playwriting and technical problems, history of the theatre and of the drama, experimental production, acting, costuming, voice and diction, radio writing and production. The consequence is that this program is preparing pupils not merely to become practicing playwrights, but to enter into various special professions connected with the drama and the theatre, the films, and the radio. No attempt at a full catalogue will be made here; but some indication will be given of some of the erroneously regarded "by-products" of the instruction of The Carolina Playmakers. To the films and the stage have gone Kay Kyser, Shepperd Strudwick, and Sidney Blackmer; to the "legitimate" stage Eugenia Rawls, Marion Tatum, Bedford Thurman, Robert Nachtmann, Elizabeth Taylor, Howard Bailey and Claudius Mintz. Lee ("P. L.") Elmore has directed many important productions, including those of Margaret Anglin for two years. Foster Fitz-Simons was associated with Ted Shawn's group of male dancers, and performed a season at The Rainbow Room in New York, toured South America, and has exhibited marked talent as stage designer. Walter Terry won the post of dance critic for the *New York Herald Tribune*. From those who hold academic positions should be singled out Hubert Heffner, who after serving here, at Wyoming, Arizona, and Northwestern University (Professor of Dramatic Literature, 1937-1938), was called to the headship of the Department of Speech and Drama at Stanford University. George V. Denny, well remembered as highly efficient publicity man for The Carolina Playmakers, served for a time on the professional stage; became director of the Institute of Arts and Sciences at Columbia University; and later, president of The Town Hall, New York

## PIONEERING A PEOPLE'S THEATRE

City, and founder of "The Town Hall of the Air," which has been signally successful.

In the contribution of The Carolina Playmakers to the field of literature may, it is suggested, be found the germs of future development in the fields of creative and critical writing—drama, novel, short story, essay, journalism and magazine writing, translation, and adaptation for stage and film, and the writing of radio plays and script. Foremost in the list of those who have achieved success in varying degrees in these fields stand: Paul Green, eminent as dramatist, novelist and short-story and film script writer; the late Thomas Wolfe, who failed to "register" as playwright, but achieved a sensational success as novelist and short story writer; and Betty Smith who, after long and pertinacious study and practice in playwriting, rang the bell, nationally, with the resounding success of the novel, "A Tree Grows in Brooklyn." Not a few Carolina Playmakers have achieved distinction, in varying degrees, as authors: Jonathan Daniels, sometime editor of *The News and Observer*, special writer for *Fortune*, author of several well-written books, and one of the confidential secretaries of President Roosevelt; Loretto Carroll Bailey, with marked gifts as playwright, whose most ambitious work was "Strike Song," written in collaboration with her husband, J. O. Bailey, professor of English here; Bernice Kelly Harris, author of a number of folk-plays and of two novels of rural life in North Carolina which won considerable acclaim, "Purslane" and "Portulaca"; Noel Houston, successful professional writer for national magazines; William Woods, whose interesting novel, "The Age of Darkness," was recently filmed, with Walter Huston in the leading role; Howard Richardson, whose promising play "The Dark of the Moon" is now playing in New York; and not a few others of varying gifts as writers in various fields, including Gwen Pharis Ringwood whose plays have won praise, prizes, and productions; Frances Gray, talented as actress and poet; Joseph Mitchell, sophisticated writer for *The New Yorker* and author of "McSorley's Wonderful Saloon," Wilbur Stout, director of the college theatre at Mississippi Southern College, Howard Bailey, member of the faculty of Rollins College, and Frederick H. Koch, Jr., director of college dramatics at Miami University.

Somewhat more than thirty-five years ago, the late Walter Hines Page, distinguished writer and editor, and later to become Ambassador at the Court of St. James's, urged Edwin Mims, who had just come here as professor of English, to "grow a crop of effective writers, start a new, great educational movement, give literary studies a new meaning and a new vitality . . ." The basic principle was thus stated by Page: "The way to teach literature is to teach men to write and to talk." It is not too late to take Page's advice and to follow his counsel of perfection. If the so-called "by-products" of the instruction of The Carolina Playmakers have been measurably conspicuous, as just indicated, there is reason to surmise that the time has come for the establishment of a school of creative and critical writing, expression, speech, and diction, in which the departments of English, dramatic art and literature, journalism and expression might co-operatively unite. The fulfilment of Page's dream is clamoring for realization.

## VI

Thus far, The Carolina Playmakers, under the leadership of Koch, Green, Selden, and their able co-adjutors, have been creatively influential and nationally pervasive in directing attention to sources of native inspiration in the fields of folk literature and Afro-American social and sociological conditions and phenomena. Hatcher Hughes' "Hell Bent for Heaven," Roark Bradford's "Green Pastures" and innumerable short stories of Negro life and character, "Porgy" and other successful dramas and stories of Dorothy and DuBose Heyward, the writings of Carl Carmer, Erskine Caldwell's "Tobacco Road" as dramatized by Jack Kirkland, Lynn Riggs' "Green Grow the Lilacs" in its smashingly successful adaptation, "Oklahoma," Maxwell Anderson's "Winterset," Robert Sherwood's "Abe Lincoln in Illinois," Lulu Vollmer's "Sun-Up," and Eugene O'Neill's "All God's Chillun Got Wings," as arresting examples, testify to the vitality and far-reaching influence of the thrust toward native sources of fictive and dramatic inspiration. In this creative illumination of fecund origins and sources, Chapel Hill has been a radiating center of high voltage. These words from an editorial in *Holland's Magazine* (July, 1936), which may slightly transgress the bounds of realistic critical appraisal, nevertheless testify eloquently to the opinion entertained by not a few competent judges of the value of the work and influence of the late Frederick Henry Koch:

"His wide influence—not for a long time yet to be fully assayed—has spread indubitably into the associated fields of the novel, the short story, and even non-fiction works. From the basic idea underlying his work and philosophy stem such writings as those of Caldwell, Heyward, Miller, Bradford, Faulkner, Stribling, and other and younger novelists. Not that many more influences have not impinged sharply and deeply on Southern writers and on Southern thought generally; but Frederick Koch and his example have been a centralizing, crystallizing, and vitalizing force unequaled in Southern literature to date."

# First Stage and First Theatre
## Of The Carolina Playmakers
### By Frederick Koch

### I

EFORE the coming of The Carolina Playmakers there was no stage designed for dramatic performance at the University of North Carolina. Each year the dramatic club put on a play in Gerrard Hall, one of the oldest buildings on the campus. But Gerrard Hall had no stage, only a lecture platform about eight inches above the floor.

"How did you manage to stage plays here?" I inquired.

"Well, we built a temporary platform over the front row of seats and strung a curtain across; the actors dressed in the Y.M.C.A. building across the way and got onto the stage through the window there."

I gasped.

"Is this the only way you have of staging plays? How do you manage rehearsals when Gerrard Hall is used for chapel exercises every day? You can't very well leave your furniture and properties around, can you?"

Looking back now, I salute those pioneering players who produced plays on this makeshift stage with all-male casts—for there were no coeds then—and who even carried their productions to neighboring towns on occasion.

I investigated all the buildings on the campus but none afforded even a platform suitable for dramatic purposes. I was discouraged. But only for a moment. As to so many other desperate directors who have had nothing to begin with, an idea came. And it proved to be a good one.

A new public school building, several blocks off the campus unfortunately, had just been completed; and it contained a comfortable auditorium with a fairly good platform-stage.

"This will do," I said. And the village officials agreed.

So we extended the apron stage into the auditorium and designed an attractive proscenium arch, a canopy over the stage, and a matching curtain of lovely brown rep bearing the newly-designed mask of The Carolina Playmakers. Fortunately my early experimentation with the same problem at the

## FIRST STAGE AND FIRST THEATRE

frontier University of North Dakota served admirably as a model. With the collaboration of various departments of the University, as in Dakota, the new Carolina stage was equipped with homemade footlight troughs, tin-can spots, and a stationary framework for hanging the scenery. We got the cheapest kind of cotton sheeting we could buy and sewed the strips together to make the three walls of the log cabin set for the first play, *When Witches Ride* by Elizabeth Lay. The walls were mounted on battens and hung like window shades. At the corners, the "canvases" were tacked to the two-by-four supports. The tacking and hammering, and the bumping and hoisting of the heavy rollers in the change of sets prolonged the intermissions to such an extent that I was called upon to talk to fill in the time. Elizabeth Lay says this got me into the bad habit of long curtain speeches on tour to help the audience forget those distracting sounds and the long intermissions.

The whole enterprise in the making of our first stage, aspiringly dubbed "The Play-House," was entirely a communal affair. As I write this I have before me the playbill of the original production of our first Carolina Folk Plays, and I note that the executive staff for the opening production included the names of twenty-eight volunteer workers of the University staff and of the village community. It was a happy gang—"an institution of the dear love of comrades" in the inimitable phrase of Walt Whitman. "The Play-House" was designed to make Chapel Hill a creative center of folk play-making in North Carolina. It served for seven years in those brave new days as a temporary home for The Playmakers.

Of course, there were many problems and not a few headaches in those first years. Boys and girls shouting and playing in the halls at recess time and broad-jumping overhead were distracting enough. But the problem of furniture and properties was the limit! They were constantly out of place—or even missing altogether. It's a wonder we ever got a show on. But somehow we did, and survived. . . .

All manner of strange parcels arrived in the village Post Office: scenic paints, gelatine color sheets, electrical switches and plugs, etc., etc. I shall never forget an express parcel of gelatine color sheets addressed to "Miss Caroline Playmaker"!

I wish I could pass on to you the thrill of the moment when the new plays came to life. The initial playbill of the opening curtain on that memorable first night of March 14, 1919 included Thomas Wolfe's first play and first published work, *The Return of Buck Gavin,* with Tom himself in the title rôle of a mountain outlaw. Here was something new and strange and wonderful! Life itself that moves and feels.

Then came *The Last of The Lowries* by Paul Green of Harnett County, a story of the Carolina Croatan outlaw, Henry Berry Lowrie, who carried seventy pounds of firearms on his person, and on whose head there was a reward of $50,000.

Soon followed in the first year a little play called *Peggy*, a tragedy of tenant farm life by Harold Williamson of Carthage in eastern Carolina. Here the drab tenant cabin we had passed a thousand times as a dull sight revealed for the first time the stark tragedy of the forgotten sharecropper. It was the forerunner of Erskine Caldwell's *Tobacco Road!* Then came Wilbur Stout's little comedy of a country courtship in the piedmont, *In Dixon's Kitchen*, which everybody loved.

Always there was an expectant and eager audience for the new plays. On the little homemade stage the earliest Carolina Folk Plays were first revealed. That was twenty-five years ago now as time runs. . . .

## II

The work grew. Still the Playmakers had no home on the campus. On every side we heard, "Get your plays out into the State and the people will see that you get a theatre."

So we toured. In the first seven years we carried our little homespun plays to every corner of North Carolina. One editor wrote, "The homefolks took to the homemade drama as to homemade sausage and corn cakes on a frosty morning." The plays found an eager audience wherever we went. The people knew them for their own.

That's how in 1925 the University Trustees voted unanimously to give The Playmakers one of the oldest and most cherished buildings on the campus, Smith Hall. Of historic tradition and classic design, Smith Hall, erected in 1850 as The Ballroom of the University, was the scene of many festive occasions. It was renamed Smith Hall because of the public sentiment against dancing. In 1885 the building was taken over by the Library, the basement serving as the chemistry laboratory and the University bathhouse! Later it was occupied by the College of Law. In 1925 the lawyers occupied a new building just completed for them and Smith Hall became The Playmakers Theatre; the first building in America to be dedicated to the making of its own native drama.

The University Trustees appropriated $25,000 to remodel Smith Hall

## FIRST STAGE AND FIRST THEATRE

as a theatre. The little building lent itself admirably to the reconstruction. But the appropriation was not sufficient to furnish the theatre. We found it would take $13,000 still to supply seating, lighting, and stage equipment.

Remembering the enthusiasm for our work of the veteran American dramatist, Augustus Thomas, I went to New York to place the problem before him. He introduced me to Frederick Keppel, President of the Carnegie Corporation. Mr. Keppel listened with interest to the story of our folk playmaking and said that he would place the matter before his Board of Directors. Discouraged, I went back to Mr. Thomas.

"I'm afraid I failed; Mr. Keppel didn't promise to *do* anything."

"I guess you didn't fail," in a kindly voice, "we'll just have to wait and see."

The following spring while I was on tour with The Playmakers in Charlotte, came a telegram from President Chase, "CHECK FOR $13,000 RECEIVED FROM CARNEGIE CORPORATION FOR PLAYMAKERS THEATRE."

On November 23, 1925 The Playmakers Theatre was dedicated with the Sixteenth Series of Carolina Folk Plays. The great crystal chandelier sparkled. Appropriately the opening curtains revealed a romance of college youth in '61, *Out of The Past by* Frances Gray of Raleigh. The play recalled the last dance held in the Ballroom before the outbreak of the War Between the States. The setting was the moonlit portico of the old building itself. The music of the waltz and the gay laughter of the dancers came from within. It was interrupted suddenly by the excited entrance of an old Negro slave, with the startling news, "Sumter is fired!" And the last dance ended in the historic Ballroom until the University was reopened five years later.

That night President Harry Woodburn Chase dedicated the building as The Playmakers Theatre "in the confidence that it may make possible about our common life a little more of the stuff that dreams are made of; that its existence here shall mean a little less monotony, a little more glamor about our days; that the horizons of imagination shall by its presence here be enlarged so that we shall come more steadily and wholly to see the place of beauty and of its handmaiden, art, in a civilization not too much given to its encouragement. To such purposes this building, the first permanent provision for any of the fine arts at the University, is from this night set apart."

The work of The Playmakers expanded, and a separate Department of

Dramatic Art was created by the University in 1936. The little Playmakers Theatre has become altogether inadequate for our rapidly widening activities. We are looking forward now to a Dramatic Art Building on the campus, and we are making definite plans for erecting such a building in the near future. One of the Foundations, which has generously helped in developing the work of the Department, is holding for us a gift of $150,000 toward this building as an endowment, with the condition that the University raise $450,-000. The University has undertaken to raise this sum of money and has affirmed its intention to do so.

Such is our dream of widening horizons.

## The Battle Cry of the Western Theatre

> For here once walked the men of dreams,
> The sons of hope and pain and wonder,
> Upon their foreheads truth's bright diadem,
> The light of sun in their countenance,
> And their lips singing a new song—
> A song for ages yet unborn,
> For us the children that came after them—
> "O new and mighty world to be!"
> They sang,
> "O land majestic, free, unbounded!"

Such a song was never sung by any of the characters, or any of the choruses created by Aeschylus, Sophocles or Euripides. The lyrical cry in Classical tragedy was a high lament for intense but will-less suffering. The cry in Western Theatre is a battle cry, a hymn celebrating the fighting search for something afar off, not easily attained—maybe never to be attained directly —but something the steady striving for which keeps every muscle taut and the blood surging victoriously.

—Samuel Selden (quoting from the Prologue to *The Lost Colony*). "*The Lost Colony* and the Greeks." Souvenir Program, 1939.

# From Script To Stage
## *Experimental Production of New Plays*
### By Edward Muschamp

The idea of presenting new plays for an actively critical audience is, we believe, distinctively a development of The Carolina Playmakers. It is interesting to trace its beginnings in this extract from a posthumously published article written by Thomas Wolfe. (The article was unfinished, and was called, when first published in the March, 1943, issue of *The Carolina Play-Book*, "The Man Who Lives with His Idea.")

When a student completes a play in Mr. Koch's course it is subjected to the "round-table criticism" in which all the members of the class take part. The class is seated around a large table, every effort being made to give an informal atmosphere to the class meetings. The play is read by the author and is then criticised by each member of the class. Mr. Koch puts great dependence on the opinion of the students in the discussions, and the revisions that are made in the play after it is first read to the class are usually the direct result of student criticism. "I find the student to be the best critic in the long run," he says. "It is true they know little of dramatic technique as 'it is done' today, but on the other hand they are not hidebound by form and their criticisms are usually real and just."

About two dozen plays were written before Christmas in 1918 by Mr. Koch's first class. Three of these were selected finally for production after an "author's reading" had been held which was open to the attendance of the student body. The author's reading, another feature of the Playmakers' method, was attended by a large number of students and they voted by ballot for the three plays that, in their opinion, would give the best program.

The method described herein was still in effect in 1930. In the early thirties, there was a slight change in that *all* completed manuscripts were given such production as the authors and their friends could summon, and were presented in groups of four and five on successive afternoons and evenings. From this orgiastic melée would emerge the three best plays, which were then given full production for the subscription audience. As the Dramatic Art Department grew larger, this unwieldy plan was of necessity modified; so that by the late thirties, the present scheme was reached of selecting only the three best plays twice each quarter, and giving them more ample production. The growth of the idea of audience participation is amply treated by Mr. Muschamp in the following article.

NOW IT IS A CLEAR, crisp winter evening—like a crisp October evening in Maine. But in the Piedmont section of North Carolina in the clear, crisp winter evening the light of a million stars twinkles down through the stark outlines of the great oak trees that mark the campus of the University of North Carolina in Chapel Hill, as students, townsfolk, and guests at the Inn hurry along the gravel paths

⁅ Edward Muschamp, well known Philadelphia journalist.

## PIONEERING A PEOPLE'S THEATRE

in the direction of The Playmakers Theatre. For "Proff" Koch and several picked groups of his students are putting on one of his now justly-famous evenings of "Experimental Productions of New Plays," wherein the audience in a good-natured but very-much-in-earnest way locks horns with the playwright. And every man, woman, and child in the theatre may for the "speaking up" become "Mr. First Nighter" himself and tell the author just what he likes about the play, and exactly what he does not like; and the author, in turn, may accept the criticism, or reject it—as he sees fit, and defend himself and his actors accordingly.

But step lively, folks, for if you don't get in the theatre early you not only won't get a seat, but all the S. R. O., will be gone, and so will all the "choice seats" on the steps! For these evenings of "Experimental Plays" have become one of the most intriguing features of Chapel Hill life, and, what is of even greater consequence, potentially one of the most important developments in the cultural and educational life of the nation. True, they cannot yet be counted as a serious rival, in popular appeal, to a Duke-Carolina football contest! But it is quite within the realm of the possible that in the not-so-very-distant years to come, when the world's bayonets and bombers are again beaten into plow-shares and commercial transport planes, and mankind has once more settled down to the enjoyment of the more humane art, what Proff Koch, and his colleagues and students in the Department of Dramatic Art of the University are doing today, may have a more beneficial and more lasting effect on the pleasurable life of the nation than all the football games that have ever been played in Chapel Hill, the Yale Bowl, and the Rose Bowl all rolled into one. For it is a conservative statement that the dramatic department of the University of North Carolina—working through these evenings of "Experimental Plays," which constitute the spear-head of its general work—is laying the foundations for a crop of American playwrights and an era of playwriting that hold infinite possibilities for the future of the American theatre and all that may mean to the future entertainment and culture of the American people. All of which is based, in a sense, on the assumption that the legitimate stage in America is far from dead; and that, offered really good plays well acted and at admission prices that are within the pocketbook reach of the average family, the American people will again flock to the theatre as they used to do before the advent of that form of public entertainment sometimes known as "movin' pit-tures."

But hurry you must, folks, or as we warned you, you won't even get standing space. Its only a little after seven and every seat in The Playmakers Theatre is already occupied, and more people are coming in.

### Enter Proff Koch

Presently the figure of a youngish looking middle-aged man—his dark hair plentifully streaked with gray, smiling, garbed in his customary Norfolk suit, and holding his pipe in one hand, stands up—down by the footlights, and announces, "We are about to begin the 80th series of Experimental Productions of New Plays, written and directed by students in the University's playwriting course"; and, with only an occasional exception, wherein a part is taken by one of the townsfolk of Chapel Hill who has been called in to complete the cast, the acting also is done by University students.

The speaker, of course, is Frederick H. Koch, head of the University's dramatic department, and founder and director of The Carolina Playmakers—one of the best known and most capable of college theatrical organizations, the sponsoring group through which the "Experimental Plays" are given. But only on the most formal occasions is he so introduced. To the more than 5,000 students at Chapel Hill, and to all the thousands who have studied there some twenty-odd years, and in professional and amateur circles throughout the nation—from Times Square to the proverbial Podunk, he is simply and affectionately known as "Proff" Koch—although there are those who insist that the correct spelling is "Proff," others persist in writing it "Proph" by way of proclaiming Koch's prophetic quality along with his other talents. But "Prof," "Proff," or "Proph," whichever the genial Koch is, he continues—as he looks up over the hill-side of occupied seats that rise tier upon tier to the uppermost reaches of the Theatre—not unlike the seats in a medical students' surgical clinic: "The author of our first play this evening is Barry Farnol, of Chicago. He's right here beside me, and he's going to tell you just why he wrote it the way he did; and after his play has been performed, and the curtain is down, he'll be back here again to face the music of your criticism and comments which he will be very glad to hear. Barry, the 'platform' is all yours."

The young playwright stands up, is greeted by a round of friendly applause, makes his brief statement concerning his play, and "ducks" down into the pit and to the stage, for as it happens in this particular instance, the author is not only directing the production and performance of his play but is also acting one of the parts. A moment later the curtain goes up and

## PIONEERING A PEOPLE'S THEATRE

the play is on. Twenty minutes or so later the last lines have been spoken, the curtain is down, the applause has come to the last hand clap. Proff Koch is again standing, smiling and looking up at the audience, and beside him stands young Mr. Farnol ready and anxious to "take his medicine"—for it is direct audience reaction to his playwriting efforts, and he knows that—however good his play may look on paper—if he has not "sold" it to his audience, he has not succeeded. Moreover, he knows that under Proff Koch's stimulating encouragement at previous Experimental Plays, his auditors will feel absolutely free to speak their honest opinions—be they critical or complimentary.

### The Audience Takes a Hand

"Well, folks," the Proff begins, "how did you like it? Is it a good play or is it a bad play? Is the plot clear or is it too involved? Did Barry make his points, or did he muff them? He told you before the curtain went up just what he had in mind when he wrote his play; now he wants to know how well he succeeded in getting his idea across the footlights. For after all is said and done, a play, you know, isn't really a play until it has registered in the minds of the audience. In other words, the drama is a social not a solitary act. It comes alive only through the response of the audience. It would be safe to wager that if there were no audience, the drama would not long survive; for in the final analysis, drama is the response of an audience to the actors' embodiment of the playwright's design. Or, if you will grant me just a moment or two more, the final test of a play lies in its appeal to an audience; hence these experimental productions of our best student-written plays, with the audience playing a direct and active part in the program. Audience participation in the play, you know, harks back to the good old days of the Greeks and the Elizabethans, and to the boos, hisses, whistles, and foot-stamping of the Nineteenth century. But in *our* experimental theatre it is a new kind of participation in which each one of you may become a critic, giving your honest impression of the play to the new playwright. . . . Now, then, how about it, George"—the Proff is now directing a question specifically to a senior who is not studying in the dramatic department but who is known to be interested in the theatre and is a regular attendant at the Experimental Plays. "What do you think of this first play of the evening? What are your reactions to it?"

"Well Proff," the senior begins, rising as he speaks, "he's got a corking good idea for his plot, and on the whole I think he's done a good job with

## FROM SCRIPT TO STAGE

it. But the 'conversion' of the principal character—toward the end of the play—his realization that he has completely misjudged the attitude of the people of his town, is too sudden, I think; it came too quickly. I realize, of course, that the action, or the dialogue, or whatever you call it, can't be too drawn out as you come to the climax of the play. But it wasn't clear to me why the old man changed so suddenly, and I was just wondering whether that point couldn't be cleared up in some way. I don't know anything about the technique of playwriting, but—"

"And yet, after all George," interrupts Proff Koch goodnaturedly, "you are potentially the fellow who walks up to the Box Office and lays down the cash for two aisle seats! And if you don't like the play, or feel that it has been marred, or weakened, by the playwright's failure to make the denouement perfectly clear, you are not going to be very enthusiastic about it, or recommend it to your friends. Your point, if it is sound, is a very practical one, and I wonder how many others in the audience feel the same way."

Then Proff asks for a show of hands—pro and con. By this time the discussion is on in full force. Some in the audience agree with George, others do not. Over here, a woman has gained recognition from Proff Koch, and is voicing her criticism, altogether different from George's. She thinks there are too many extraneous characters, that they are confusing, and that if a couple of them were eliminated, and the time that they consume given to additional lines for the "old man" and his "niece," the plot would be perfectly clear and the play improved one hundred per cent. From one of the "standees" at the back of the theatre comes the comment that too many of the "lines" are "speeches," and all the play needs is to break the "speeches" up into more dialogue. And so it goes. The young playwright smiles, and is serious, as from time to time he speaks up to defend or explain his technique and method.

Word reaches Proff Koch from "back stage" that "time is up" and the next play is ready to go on. He and the young playwright thank the audience for their interest and participation in the discussion; there is another round of applause, and—"the show goes on!" At the conclusion of the second Experimental Play there is another "friendly autopsy" or "inquest," as it were; and so on until the conclusion of the evening's program.

### How the Plan Works

The evolution of these "Experimental Productions" is a remarkable story in itself, and is based on the Koch dictum that "a play is not a play until it is produced and until an audience has reacted to it"—a fact that professional producers know all too well from many costly and bitter experiences. And it is by no means too exaggerated a statement to say that had Broadway the facilities for doing exactly what Proff Koch is doing in his Experimental Productions, Broadway might be saved many dollars and many heartbreaks. Nor is it unreasonable to assume, by the same token, that out of Koch's work may come a crop of American playwrights that, guided and tempered in the furnace of Experimental Productions, will possess a fundamental understanding of what constitutes successful playwriting, and, an equipment for doing such work, that may lead the way to a genuine renaissance of the American theatre. Indeed there are not a few persons who feel that the renaissance is already underway and that Koch and the work he is doing are playing a very definite part in the development; for as one critic has written of the plays produced in the Chapel Hill class rooms: "They have a spark, a glow of life and they ring true. . . . Their real significance lies not only in their relation to the now flourishing little theatre movement, but as trail-blazers for such plays as *The Green Pastures, In Abraham's Bosom, Abe Lincoln in Illinois, Our Town, Winterset,* and *Tobacco Road.*

But, to record this evolution, briefly: it began with a student-author sitting at a bare kitchen table in an ordinary room reading his play before a committee of judges—such committees being composed of various members of the University faculty, who at the conclusion of the reading engaged in a free-for-all discussion of the play. Before long it was decided to invite such of the public as might be interested, to attend these readings—but the public's job was merely to sit and listen, and say nothing! Then it occurred to Koch that it would probably be much more interesting and bring out more of the play-manuscript if they held what he called "script performances." That is to say, the various parts in a play were assigned to various student-actors, and they in turn read the parts. But in these "script performances," much of an advance over the original readings as they were, there were no costumes, no make-up, and no scenery, and the slim audiences—for up to this time these embryonic "experimental productions" had failed to arouse very much public interest—continued to sit "mute and inglorious." Just the same, it was quite perceptible that these "script performances" marked a definite advance over the original authors' readings. So Koch said: "Fine, but let's go a step further. Let's see what we've got in the way of odds and ends of costumes and scenery that we've used in some of our regular plays, that we can now use again to 'back up' these script readings without spending any time or money on the work." Thus another step forward was recorded. And then realizing how much the makeshift costumes and scenery were adding to the performances, it was decided that it would be well worth while to provide costumes and scenery to fit specifically each new experimental play. But still the public was permitted to do no more than to listen—to "lay low" and say "nothin'." Finally Koch said to himself one day: "If these really are 'experimental' plays, and I am right in my theory that a play is not a play until it has been performed before an audience, and the audience has reacted to what has transpired on the stage, why not invite the audience to participate in the performance? Why not ask the audience to 'speak right out in meeting'—as it were, while the production is still 'warm,' and discover just what these folks out there on the other side of the footlights think of the play, and learn what they like, and what they don't like, and why."

So, the first completely evolutionized "Experimental Production of New Plays" at the University of North Carolina came into being, and the Koch "revolution" in the process of teaching young men and young women to write and produce plays, had triumphed. Once again the zig-zag and multifarious "story of mankind" had taken a positive and forward step.

## Our Way of Playwriting

I believe that when the Good Book says "God created man in His own image," it means that God imparted to man somewhat of his own creativeness; in a sense He made man a co-worker with Him — potentially an artist! In our way of playwriting we try to cherish the creative spark of the student. We encourage him to examine, with understanding and imagination, the eventful happenings of his own experience, the characters of his own neighborhood. Then we guide him in shaping his materials in an appropriate and interesting pattern for the stage.

—Frederick H. Koch. Introduction to *American Folk Plays.*

# Dramatic Art in a University Program

By Samuel Selden

### Art or Education?

ONCE a year, on a late December afternoon, the university Professor of Drama locks the door of his office, packs his suitcase, and boards a train for New York to attend a conference of the National Theatre Association. There for three exciting days he forgets his world of lectures, term papers, and departmental reports and thinks only of a world of art.

At night, perhaps he goes to view a new play by John Van Druten. It is a sensitively drawn character study of an immigrant family in Philadelphia. The actress playing the role of the valiant mother performs her part with consummate skill, with a warm, vibrant tenderness. The other actors also are good; and everything about the external presentation—the direction, the settings, the costuming, the lighting—is eminently satisfying. The Professor, whose senses and emotions have been dulled by months of hard labor with collegiate thespians, is stirred once more into singing life. How beautiful is this institution of the Theatre! he tells himself.

The next day, at a conference meeting, he hears a leading playwright plead passionately for the preservation of the nascent arts in American life. The speaker makes reference to a "needy generation" and states the impelling opportunity the Theatre has to bring to a hungry people something of vision and faith. A director and a critic echo his words.

Then other prominent represetnatives of the Stage, together with emissaries from the Radio and Screen, address remarks directly to the university delegates. They discuss feelingly the passing of the old stock companies which once served as training schools for apprentices. Now, they say, a great void exists. Young actors, playwrights and designers have nowhere to go for their basic training. Only the university departments of drama can supply this lack. Therefore these departments have a high responsibility. But they cannot discharge it unless those who teach dedicate themselves to their work. Instructors in the Theatre must cease to think merely of training for appreciation and give thought to the quality of their students' products; they must establish stricter standards; they must be satisfied with nothing less than perfection. University students of Dramatic Art should be equipped to stand at the forefront of the embattled lines of the Theatre, and they can do this only when they themselves are imbued with an uncompromising ambition.

The atmosphere of the conference is heady. The Professor is still affected by its spell as he sits in his Pullman seat on the way home. He keeps thinking of the remarks of the Playwright, and he repeats over and over to himself the last words of that address: "In the temple of drama the 'non-professional' has no place. Every aim, every standard must be, in the best sense of the term, 'professional.' . . . One art—one Theatre—indivisible!"

The Professor ponders his own work at the university. He has labored hard. Yet the results seem in many ways dissatisfying. Why? He has spread his time and the time of his colleagues over too many minor activities, perhaps. The members of the Department have lost themselves in a maze of petty academic chores. Consequently they, together with the students they are teaching, have lost the vision of their work. Well, that must stop. Hereafter, the Professor decides, there must be more singleness of purpose. Everyone, faculty member and assistant, and plain buck student must strive with new effort for a Theatre of standards. Hereafter, no compromises! Work! Work as never before!

### The Perch on the Fence

Full of bright confidence in the new prospects, the Professor walks next morning into his office. On his desk he finds a letter from the Dean:

"There seems to be a growing disposition on the part of students in the Department of Drama to spend a disproportionate part of their time in stage activities to the detriment of their studies in other fields. We hope that this situation can be adjusted at once. . . . This letter is not meant to be a criticism of your program, but I do wish to call attention to the fact that our theory has always been that we should not develop in the direction of the conservatory type of education."

The Professor of Drama sits for a long time staring at the letter. First he is stunned, then a little angry. Then a strange kind of shame creeps over him. He has been dreaming beautiful, but foolish, dreams, and he has been caught at it. He should know better than to do that—at his age! Yes, the Dean is quite right. The Professor's department is part of a General College of Arts and Sciences, and as such it should concern itself primarily with basic education, not technical training. Fair-haired playwrights have persuasive tongues! Maybe what they say makes sense when addressed to the right people, but they have mighty little understanding of the requirements, and the limitations, of collegiate programs!

Already the beautiful words uttered at the conference have begun to fade. The Professor likes teaching in a university community, and he is quite willing to view his specialty of the theatre as a cultural curriculum only. All right, from now on no Art, just Education.

But then he is assailed by a strange new doubt. He has turned his back on one area of activity. Now, can he and his department legitimately be regarded as having a place in the other? Does a dramatic curriculum really belong in Education? he asks himself. He believes—or he wants with all his heart to believe—that it does, but he has difficulty finding the absolute proof he desires to bolster his faith in that position. The casual evidence, at least, seems to weigh against him. The Professor remembers his last three experiences with the Divisional Committee to which he presented requests for an extension of credit on certain basic Theatre courses. After much debate the members of the Committee granted his requests, but with obvious reluctance. The term "skill courses" was used frequently, and at one point the chairman sighed. "If we permit our programs to be cluttered by very many more of these technical courses without content," he remarked drily, "I can see the death of the humanities."

Technical courses without content! Suddenly a bitter feeling of frustration sweeps over the Professor. What is he anyhow? To his mind comes the figure of a queer creature he has seen once in a cartoon. It is a Mugwump, a sad bird doomed to sit forever high on a fence between two green gardens, with its mug on one side and its wump on the other—and unable to reach the ground on either side.

### Facing the Predicament

The peculiarly exalted position of the academic Mugwump makes him an unhappy individual. He has no liking for his elevated perch, he hates to be divided, and the direction of his posture fills him with acute embarrassment. Viewing with equal yearning the gardens 'aft and 'fore his place on the fence, he is distressed by the fact that he must point his wump at one of them.

The Mugwump is not only a sad bird, he is also a lonely one—or that is how he usually sees himself. The truth is that his species is numerous. If he once lifts his eyes from his own misery he is apt to discover that neighboring fences are full of companions. The sight of all those self-divided birds sitting in melancholy gloom high on their drafty perches would be a tragic one if it were not so ridiculous.

It is my conviction that most of the Mugwump's anguish springs from causes which originate in his own mind. The fence which elevates him above the ground where he would like to be is, to a considerable extent at least, a psychological one. The primary reasons for his predicament are threefold: the Mugwump does not really understand the areas of Art and Education he yearns to possess, he lacks the courage to declare his right to occupy them—not one, but both of them—and he suffers from the delusion that any barrier set up between them is indissoluble.

In the following pages of this article I want to examine the first and third points in the Mugwump's problem with the purpose of showing that the Professor of Drama can rightly claim a place in both Art and Education, and that there need not be any fence between them.

### Professional Training and Liberal Training

First, I want to state my premise: that is, that fair-haired playwrights need not necessarily be regarded as impractical dreamers, and fast-talking emissaries from the world of Commercial Theatre may speak sense. Theatre, in the broad meaning of that term which includes Radio and Film together with the Stage, is today the most lively, if not the most extensive, agency in the country for the communication and dissemination of ideas. Nightly, literally tens of millions of minds are affected by its spell. Thus Dramatic Art, dynamically stimulating by its very nature, exerts an almost fearfully powerful force on the development of the cultural life of America. The University which is interested in exploiting every implement for education available cannot reasonably ignore the resources of the Theatre.

If the University has a stake in the Theatre, the reverse is also true. The Theatre needs the help of the University men and women. The stock companies are dead. There are now almost no dramatic conservatories which offer anything beyond the most elementary training. The majority of them limit their appeal quite frankly to star-struck youths and debutantes. More and more, therefore, the Stage, Radio, and Films have been forced in recent years to turn for apprenticeship material—though they have often been reluctant to admit it—to the Community Playhouses, but particularly to the

## PIONEERING A PEOPLE'S THEATRE

University Departments of Drama. This is especially true in the fields of writing, but it is also true in acting, directing and designing.

The University which desires to associate itself practically with the Theatre must do so fearlessly. Courses merely in the appreciation of Dramatic Art cannot carry much influence except to those persons who wish to watch the ceaseless game of action from the sidelines. When the University determines to exert its influence aggressively it must train people with dedicated minds and able hands ready to take an actual part in creative work. But it must train them well, for the world of Theatre is keenly competitive, a world in which good intentions unsupported by expert knowledge of mediums stand no chance of employment whatsoever.

A curriculum of specialized training for those who wish seriously to become professional craftsmen on the Stage, in Radio or Films—or in the fields of Community Theatre or Recreation—has, I believe, a thoroughly legitimate place in a University program. A Department of Drama which does not seek adequate equipment and qualified personnel for at least some specialized instruction in Art is, it seems to me, missing an important opportunity.

However, the Department which regards *all* of its work as specialized is as wrong as that one which ignores advanced training entirely. The Department which sets itself up to be a conservatory primarily is headed for certain trouble. The end is usually suicide.

First of all, the assumption that all those who enroll in such a Department are worthy of advanced training is untenable. The really talented student, the one who can rightfully be encouraged to direct his ambitions toward earning a living in the precarious world of Art, is a rare one. To turn the thoughts of the manifestly ungifted even for a moment toward this goal is criminal. Out of a yearly enrollment of perhaps fifty or seventy-five intelligent young men and women, the Department would be fortunate if it could honestly recommend a small dozen for the professional courses.

But this does not mean that all the others should be discouraged from studying Dramatic Art. To do that would be to deny the value of dramatic study as liberal education. The Professor of Theatre who is ever doubtful about this should resign from his Department and go into other work. I am fully convinced that Dramatic Art, rightly taught, is as stimulating, informative, and illuminating and has—potentially, at least—as much "content" as English, History, Language, and Philosophy.

Concerning the several courses in Dramatic Literature and History in the

## DRAMATIC ART IN A UNIVERSITY PROGRAM

Department's curriculum, there is seldom any question raised. They are filled to the brim with subject matter generally recognized as sound. What are commonly challenged by outsiders are the so-called "practical" courses, such as Acting, Directing, Playwriting, Scenery and Lighting. Although these are respected as useful disciplines for students desiring to develop techniques, they are suspected of having little to offer beyond mere skill. When the courses are carefully examined, however, they can usually prove themselves to be among the most truly "liberal" parts of the whole Dramatic program.

The common opposition to the "skill" courses springs from an ignorance of what they actually include. One of the least understood is Acting. By most persons acquainted only with high-school commencement plays and other informal theatricals, learning to act involves three things: the conquest of stage fright, learning how to move without stumbling over other people's feet, and acquiring enough lung power to blast one's words to the rear of the auditorium. Useful as these specific "skills" may be to the egocentric student who wishes to display himself in grease paint, they may indeed have little to offer in general education.

If a University course in Acting covered these three points only, the critics would probably be right in questioning the place of such a study in a liberal arts program. Actually, however, a well-set-up course in Acting covers far more territory than that indicated. It stresses from the beginning a careful study of people. The course begins with a sociological investigation of the personalities who compose the audience. The student examines the organization of the community which surrounds the spectators, and then these spectators' conditioned desires in the playhouse for diversion, for stimulation, and for illumination of their daily lives. Thus from the very start the apprentice actor is taught to view his art in terms of a relationship and responsibility.

The second phase of the work is concerned with the study and exercise of the whole body in order to make it a vibrantly expressive instrument—not for use in the theatre only, but everywhere. Careful attention is given to good posture and to the development of a strong, but flexible and sensitive, control of every part of the physical, vocal, and mental organism. In subsequent lecture and practice periods the actor is taught to see clearly each of the several factors in typical human situations (off the stage as well as on) which force a person into a responsive attitude; and then the actor is encouraged to experiment freely with the actions which grow out of those attitudes so that he may understand why people—and therefore players—behave the way they do in different circumstances.

This is only the beginning. More complex problems arise to be solved when the student starts to interpret actual passages of dialogue, and particularly when he tries to analyze, visualize, and construct a living characterization. Throughout his course he has been taught the value of alertness, preparedness, and dependability, and he has had rigorous practice in thinking beyond himself into the minds of his dramatic team-mates and the minds of the people seated out front.

Not all effective courses in Acting have identical programs, of course, but the fundamentals are the same. A student who completes his work in any of them has had skill training. At the same time he has had something more. He has advanced his appreciation of both the thought and the language of dramatic literature, he has exercised his knowledge of human psychology, and he has learned to be expressive.

Similar claims can be made for every other course in the "skill" group. Playwriting involves practice in setting speeches together in such a way as to make a reading of them "sound like easy, natural conversation." But Playwriting also demands research and analysis in human behavior, experiments in visualization, and a careful study of problems in design. Courses in Scenery and Lighting include instruction in the manual manipulation of tools, but they also include work leading to a new appreciation of form and color, of materials, and especially of the psychological relationships between a man in action and his environment—the house he lives in, the furniture he sits on, the implements he handles. These courses of study review everything the student has learned elsewhere about physics, and they encourage him to check back over his knowledge of historical materials. Courses in Speech, Directing, Costuming, Radio Production, and all the rest, though rightly stressing "skill," are also full of "content."

A scholarly approach to learning in any field of study demands a full use of all the tools available. The student of Classical Literature who wishes really to understand what he is reading must make himself familiar with grammar, vocabulary and verse forms. It is just as important for the student of the Literature of the Theatre to become acquainted with the dynamic structure of his subject. Drama is the art of "doing something," in motion. Manifestly that means acting, setting and lighting. As absurd as trying to study music without a concert hall is trying to study plays without a stage. Here then is the primary reason for the theatre "skill" courses. They have great educational value in themselves; they have even greater value as adjuncts to the reading courses.

## The Emotions in Liberal Education

One of the greatest lessons taught us by the history of the last six years is that people are influenced in the long run less by reason than by emotion. Commentators have pointed out repeatedly that much of the bloodiest fighting has taken place between nations which before the war boasted the highest levels of literacy. Knowledge and the ability to rationalize are not wholly dependable guarantors of sanity. When the heart of man is stirred he gives little heed to his mind. Recognizing this fact, American education which, since the turn of the century had devoted its chief attention to information and rationalization, has in recent seasons begun to give consideration to problems of human feelings.

In an article entitled "Education for the Emotions" which appeared in the August 19, 1944, issue of *The Saturday Review of Literature*, George F. Reynolds points out the strategic influence which may be exerted on our feeling by the artist. He says:

"Our emotional responses are 'not Time's fools,' they are not easily changed. . . . Changes come mostly through contagion—the influence of people we admire, of new groups we become a part of. And some changes also come from the books we read, the pictures we see, the music we hear—in general, the arts we vitally experience. But the arts so subtly shift our points of view, widen our tolerances, soften our prejudices, that we often do not catch them at it. They make us laugh with people or at them, make them seem glamorous or repulsive, something to imitate or something to despise."

Although Reynolds does not here specially mention the art of the Theatre, he implies it for he mentions it elsewhere in the article. An intelligent study of the best of Dramatic Art, like that of books, pictures, and music, helps the student acquire through contacts with the emotional factors an intuitive recognition of values, a feeling for moral relationships, and a sense of unrationalized, but nevertheless valid, perspectives. An association with the forces of Drama often brings with it an illumination not acquired by any other art experience, since the Theatre possesses a third dimension in action peculiar to itself.

A perception and understanding of the emotional factors of human living (as reflected in the Drama) may be acquired to some extent in those courses which concern themselves solely with the appreciation of literature and history. Points of view are established much more firmly, however, when the strictly content courses are supplemented by practice courses in creative writing, designing, and interpretation, for then the student approaches the study of emotion, not just from the outside, but also from the inside. In these supplementary courses the student, working under supervision, actually experiences emotion. He makes it, expresses it, controls it. At every step of his work he meets the human challenge of a small representative society composed of his instructor, his fellow craftsmen, and the members of an audience. Thus he has abundant opportunity to learn firsthand what is the real meaning of such terms as "motive," "drive," "stimulus-and-response," "environmental pressures," "primitive urges," "social checks," and similar factors in behavior. Gradually, but surely, he comes to understand the difference between excitement and sentimentality on the one hand and genuine emotion on the other, the differences between momentary stimulation and long-range satisfactions. Those are the things about which plays are written.

But probably the greatest lessons in the recognition and management of emotion come in the activities outside the classroom—in rehearsal hours, in the scene shop, on the lighting crew. Here the student learns the value of personal initiative and responsibility, a respect for order, and a healthy concern for deadlines. Above all things he gets daily experience in cooperative effort similar to that required in an athletic team. He finds out just how necessary it is to plan his own contribution for a right place and a right instant, and to fit it into the master design of a group performance in such a way as not to check or distort any other part.

### Three Programs: General, Specialized, and Graduate

In the foregoing pages I have tried to explain why I believe that the University Department of Drama should claim a place in the academic areas on both sides of the Mugwump's fence, the garden of Specialized Professional Training and the garden of General, or Liberal Education. The two areas should not only exist in a friendly way side by side, they should also have access to each other; they are mutually necessary.

Without the General training, the Specialized part has little meaning. The theatre already abounds in specialists of a sort—writers, designers, actors, engineers. For that reason there would be small sense in inviting young people to come to a University community filled with rich resources of broad knowledge if they are to confine themselves after they arrive simply to grooves already well established elsewhere. What the Theatre (including Radio and Films) needs from the American University is young men and women who are generally well informed and who have learned to look at life steadily, honestly, and inquiringly without too much concern for passing fads of thought, and who then—and only then—have begun to develop certain disciplines necessary for professional employment.

Whether the time will ever come when the University-trained craftsman will be able to regard himself on graduation as a fully qualified professional is extremely doubtful. The company or studio in which he seeks employment will almost certainly wish to do the finishing job on him. But, under the right kind of tutoring during his student period he should be able to go far with his preliminary conditioning. There is a great deal of basic preparatory work he can do at the University.

If the Specialized program needs the association of the General, the converse is also true. As I have already suggested, very few of the students enrolled in the Department will be eligible for the more advanced work. Nevertheless, the "regular," or common student, who looks forward to enjoying the Theatre as avocation only, will gain much from working side by side with the student who is earnestly concerned about professional standards. The presence of the specializing students will check the development of those easy compromises which tend to creep into college dramatics, and help to maintain a healthy respect for truly ambitious effort.

The broad base, however, will always come first. The genius, if he is not to become a brilliant but impractical floater in the Theatre, must learn the values to be found in literary, historical, scientific, and esthetic research, and especially he must come to recognize the need for habits of cooperative thinking. All along the line of creation the work of the genius has to have the support of many lesser artists laboring with him. Maxwell Anderson, in a speech he made at the Founder's Day exercises at Carnegie Institute in 1937, aptly pictures the process of united labor:

"The supreme artist is only the apex of a pyramid; the pyramid itself must be built of artists and art lovers, apprentices and craftsmen so deeply imbued with a love for the art they follow or practice that it has become for them a means of communication with whatever has been found highest and most admirable in the human spirit."

Besides the General and the Specialized curricula, the University Department of Drama must give attention to a third, not yet mentioned in this article. That is the Graduate. This is, of course, that field which will be of interest primarily to the student concerned with Dramatic Literature, History, and Criticism. Most of the men and women who elect this program will be preparing themselves for teaching.

In a well-integrated plan, however, there might well be a considerable amount of overlapping between the Graduate and the Specialized curricula. If the Specialist is going to guard himself against any too-early crystalization of his working methods he will have to establish good habits of research. On the other hand, no student should be permitted to receive a graduate degree without some first-hand experience in technique. Only at the point of climax should the two programs veer away from each other.

The following diagram suggests how the three fields of Dramatic study dealt with in this article might be viewed together.

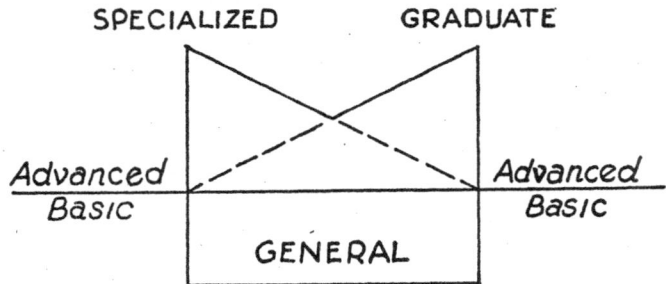

For the General and the Graduate fields of study the University already has degrees, the Bachelor's and the Master's. For the other field of Specialization there is now no degree offered in more than a very few institutions. Perhaps no degree is advisable. However, since ambitious students usually wish to have their records labeled for convenient reference when they are applying for employment, the University might grant a certificate. A student would become eligible for this special award only when in the opinion of the Dramatic faculty the quality of his work had reached a level of excellence which merited recognition. This kind of certification would encourage those who are preparing for teaching to supplement their graduate training with practice in the techniques of the Theatre, and thus fit themselves for more well-rounded service.

Thus, it seems to me to be apparent that the Mugwump's fence need not exist at all. Dramatic study belongs on both sides of the dividing line, and there is no need of a barrier if those who are planning the various curricula see clearly how they may at the same time be differentiated and integrated.

# DRAMATIC ART IN A UNIVERSITY PROGRAM

Barriers tend to rise only when instructors are uncertain in their own minds or fail to explain their purposes clearly to others.

## A Theatre of the Community

Important as the study programs are, they will occupy just a part of the attention of an active Department of Drama. The Department will give thought also to the community in which it operates.

A live University Playhouse serves the town in which it stands only when it recognizes several extramural responsibilities. It must be a general recreational center, providing good entertainment to many people. Its auditorium doors should be open to all who wish to enter, and its stage door should welcome all who wish to participate in playmaking activities. It is true that the most important work should be assigned by rights to University students seeking training, but interested persons from the town should have an opportunity to try-out for the plays and to offer their help in the scenery and costume shops.

Beyond the limits of the local town is a county and a state. For these larger territories, the University Playhouse and its staff must provide inspiration and guidance in many matters related to Dramatic activities. It should give technical advice where it is requested, help with the organization of new projects, and offer assistance in seasonal festivals.

But most of all, the University Playhouse must be an institution serving the community in the cause of the human spirit. It must be, not just a school and a theatrical agency, but also a temple of beauty. In a humble way it must strive to fulfil the responsibility suggested by President Harry Woodburn Chase when in 1925 he dedicated the Playmakers' Theatre:

"... that it may make possible about our common life a little more of the stuff that dreams are made of; that its existence here shall mean a little less monotony, a little more glamour about our days; that the horizons of imagination shall by its presence here be enlarged so that we shall come more steadily and wholly to see the place of beauty and of its handmaiden, art, in a civilization not too much given to its encouragement."

# The Lyric Lazy South

*Excerpt from a Letter to Nell Battle Lewis*

By PAUL GREEN

BUT MY thesis then as now and always will be is that we as a people, a state, nation or world will have a better chance to get out of the thick woods and night of tragedy—wasteful, perverse tragedy—when we can go beyond a belief in the almighty power and value of *things* and their money-functioning to a philosophy of their beauty and enjoyment—seeing them not as competing and fighting units and tokens in an economy of life but as instruments and means of cooperation and enlightenment among men—which is their real value after all, or they have none. Yes, the artist as prophet and statesman is what I'm talking about.

In the realm of true religion and beauty (and they both are one) the tragic dilemma of destructive and suffering man comes nearer to being dissolved away than not. Of course it can never be entirely dissolved, for man must suffer, hope and die until the end of time as he has from the blind beginning. But he can have those exquisite, isolated and mainly individual moments of vision and affirmation, and can increase those moments among his fellows. And there's where the urge and the call come in. And he can create these moments, lift himself out of the rut of a too-pragmatic and nose-to-the-grindstone existence—into another kind of existence—the kind that Socrates, Plato, Goethe, and many another follower of harmony and graciousness have talked about and worked to make prevail—can if he will.

Three hundred years ago the dreamers came into this land of ours—the rabble, the crooks, the cranks, the weak men, the idealists, the strong men, the hopeful and despairing—and all were hunting for something, something not only outside themselves but inside.

First, they conquered the wilderness.

Second, they created the democratic form of government.

Third, they led the way in the creation of the machine age.

It took them two hundred and fifty years to do these three things. My contention is that now it is up to us to do the fourth thing, to create an age of culture in the life of our country—(yes, I know that's a suspect word, but still it is the right word)—the age of art, true science, right thinking—the transfiguration of our life into terms of art, the art of living. It seems to me that one might say that it was for this very thing that our country was created. And if we fail to make our contribution in bringing it to pass just so much we fail those who struggled before us, fail the hopes and the purpose of those who come after us, and worst of all fail and betray ourselves.

We are already fifty years late!

Yes, that's what I mean—life is an art:—green winter fields in this the lyric, lazy and indulgent South; paint on the houses, flowers at the door, and care and beauty and love surrounding our bare, pitiful little country churches; lights and water and conveniences for men and their housewives, not that they may snooze the light away and grow fat in greasy ease, but that they may have more time for books and music and singing. And then outdoor plays and festivals and the beauty of maydays and the sweet and tender girl queen with the prideful young king walking by her side; and good health and joy and imagination among our children; and the poets in Lillington, little Washington, Asheville, Henderson or anywhere, writing better and better verse of their dreaming for the papers; and festivals and choruses and orchestras and so on to the mutual stimulation and give and take among us all! For these decorations of life are the inspiration, the fire, the color and drive and depthful meaning of life. And it is now no longer a matter of the pocketbook, if it ever was, but a matter of the soul. It is the soul I'm talking about.

I am talking about the soul . . . . . .

## Music in the Theatre

Everywhere there is music in America—good and bad, stimulating and deadening, enriching and pauperizing—but music just the same, waiting for its worthy and inspiring use. What of a nation with its song on every lip, with its melody in every heart, with its feet ready to move to every dance? And asking so I wonder to think that those who make the plays of men and what men do and dream should so continue their pale frustrated page and set their characters down in dry and empty wordiness. . . . It is still my belief that only in an imaginative, poetic and musical theatre can the true heart and soul of this great upsurging nation of ours find adequate and worthy dramatic state.

—Paul Green. *The Carolina Play-Book*, Vol. XII, No. 2.

# Drama In Extension

### By KAI HEIBERG-JURGENSEN

IF the Office of Defense Transportation permits, the Carolina Playmakers Theatre in Chapel Hill, N. C. will resound with young voices, earnestly declaiming the lines of plays, original and professional, for the twenty-second time in twenty-two years when The Carolina Dramatic Association holds its Annual Drama Festival and Tournament on April 12-14, this spring.

The beginnings of this organization and its wildfire growth in the State of North Carolina make a fascinating tale that sings of courage and perseverance and, above all, faith. It had its start back in 1918, when, in the Annual Report of the President of the University of North Carolina, the Director of the Bureau of Extension noted the addition to the Bureau's staff of Professor Frederick H. Koch, "who is to direct the activities of the Division of Community Drama."

Fighting for elbow-room every day of his life in North Carolina, finding one extension after another too small to satisfy his vision and ambitions, Professor Koch built dramatic activity in North Carolina until the State was called "the most theatre-going in the Union." Then he stretched the work beyond the state, flooding the entire South with his ideas until finally, one day, the American drama historian, Arthur Hobson Quinn, stood before an assemblage in Chapel Hill and said:

"Frederick H. Koch has done something which no one except himself and his pupils has been able to do, and I believe his success is due largely to his unquenchable spirit that has never been discouraged by circumstances and never truckled to anything that was base or banal in the theatre. The best way to epitomize his service is to try to imagine what the American drama would have been during the last twenty-one years without him."

That was in April, 1940, two decades after North Carolina had been described by H. L. Mencken as "the Sahara of the Bozart."

Professor Koch began his work during a period of confused ideas and tawdry values in the American theatre. Scorning imitation, he turned swiftly, innately to the people for his answer. He believed that what is essentially true of the common people in one locality is essentially true of all common people in all localities. Hence the logical attack for his ambition

## DRAMA IN EXTENSION

was a simple one. He started with the University community. When he looked beyond the campus, he continued to work with communities. After organizing several local pageants which called on the active help of large bodies of citizens, he turned his attention to the more intensive development of local drama groups. Next he promoted the writing and production of local folk plays by these groups, then tours of folk plays, and finally state-wide festivals. His emphasis throughout was on original, creative labor. Little by little, Mr. Koch won over the people of his state, and eventually the local work of North Carolina influenced the entire country.

There can be little doubt that Professor Koch's work leads toward a National Drama and a National Theatre. Naturally, he was aware of the fact that a national culture and hence a national art are based deep in the hearts of the people. If we examine the works of the great composers of every country, we find invariably back of their work a tremendous body of folk music. The dramatists and the novelists are dependent on similar materials. They go to the people of their nation for material, to the dreams and the voice of the people, and express what they find there. The road Frederick H. Koch followed led through these folk materials. Here are the steps he took:

### Pageantry

His first problem was that of reaching the common people of the State through their educators and through their community leaders; for it is the people who make a theatre and not the actors. A dozen companies of excellent actors would be of no avail without an audience and without substance for their plays. There lies the communal power of the theatre—in a participation by the people on both sides of the footlights. Mr. Koch knew this—and he also knew how to achieve this participation.

It was indeed fortunate that the city of Raleigh celebrated its three hundredth anniversary in the year 1919 and needed a Tercentenary Pageant to dramatize its history. Thus at the very beginning of his career in North Carolina, the young Professor Koch struck at the very heart of the state with his composition and production of the historical pageant, *Raleigh, the Shepherd of the Ocean*. That was the beginning of what was to become one of the most important phases of the dramatic development of North Carolina. The popularity of pageants spread like a prairie fire—pageants for every purpose, but in the main either historical or educational.

The importance of these pageants lay not in their art, but in their communal quality. They drew within their circle people from all levels of society, all working together—writing, acting, carpentering, making costumes or directing—to present the history of their community, or a dramatization of the advantages of education, or some other theme of civic importance.

The communal quality of the early pageants was advanced to real national importance in Paul Green's symphonic drama, *The Lost Colony,* as well as in his historical drama, *The Highland Call.*

*The Lost Colony* was written to celebrate the 350th anniversary of the beginning at Roanoke Island in 1587 of English colonization in America. Directed by Professor Samuel Selden, it was staged at the seaside on the original site of the landing of Sir Walter Raleigh's early colonists. In the summer of 1937 and for four following summers it drew into its activities the participation of the Federal Theatre Project, The Carolina Playmakers, the CCC boys of the Works Progress Administration, the Westminster Choir School of Princeton, N. J., and the people of Roanoke Island. Over a quarter of a million people attended.

*The Highland Call* was produced at Fayetteville October 14-November 2, 1939, to celebrate The Cape Fear Scottish Festival. The Carolina Playmakers, the local people, students from Flora Macdonald College and several professional actors all had a part in the production which was directed by John W. Parker, Field Agent for the Bureau of Community Drama.

## The Bureau of Community Drama

The avowed purpose of *The Bureau of Community Drama,* initiated in 1919, is "to promote and encourage dramatic arts in the schools, colleges, and communities of North Carolina; to meet the need for a genuinely constructive recreation; to cooperate in the production of plays, pageants, and festivals of real worth, and to stimulate interest in the writing of native drama."

After familiarizing the people with drama through the communal pageants and keeping them continually aware of it by a constant succession of speeches, addresses and lectures, Professor Koch now reached out into every corner of North Carolina through the *Bureau of Community Drama.* It offered help in the organization and productions of drama groups; gave advice as to play selection, direction, scenery construction, make-up and anything else which might fall under the heading of community drama—and offered it free of charge.

The enormous and rapid growth of the *Bureau of Community Drama* is

## DRAMA IN EXTENSION

best illustrated by noting how the demand for its services leapt forward from year to year. In 1919-20 there were calls for forty playbooks; by 1922-23 the number had jumped to 875; and in 1924-25, five years after the Bureau was founded, 2,150 playbooks were sent out to North Carolina communities.

In 1921 an *Institute for Dramatic Workers* was planned to be held annually in order to promote cooperation between independent groups of "community players." Today, twenty-four years later, this gathering still takes place every year. It is now known as the *Directors' Conference.*

Another milestone was passed with the appointment of John W. Parker as Extension Instructor in Dramatic Art in 1934. Instituting Extension courses in Play Production for the purpose of training leaders to direct dramatic activities throughout the State, teaching ever-increasing numbers of students, mailing out pamphlets and planning study-courses, Mr. Parker had developed a broad organization by the time he was called to the Army in June, 1942.

One of the most remarkable chapters in the history of the *Bureau of Community Drama* is that which records the power of survival displayed by the organization during the dark years immediately following the crash in 1929. While one activity after another was falling by the wayside, the Bureau bound up its wounds and went ahead under the direction of Professor Koch and his assistant, Mrs. Irene Fussler, both working without remuneration. It was their love of the organization and their belief in its necessity that kept it going.

### THE CAROLINA DRAMATIC ASSOCIATION

By 1922-23 so many community drama groups had developed that a more effective organization became necessary in order to render them essential aid and encouragement. For that purpose a new institution came into existence: *The Carolina Dramatic Association.*

Then again began a wildfire growth that reads like a statistical whirlwind. In 1923-24 there were thirty-two groups enrolled in the C.D.A., the next year there were fifty-two; and in 1927-28 the membership consisted of one hundred and sixteen groups.

By this time Professor Koch had advanced three steps up the ladder toward his goal: first, the *Pageants* to make the people of North Carolina drama conscious, then the *Bureau of Community Drama* to encourage these people to form permanent dramatic groups, and finally the *Carolina Dramatic As-*

*sociation* to knit these organized groups into one state-wide organization, drawing everything into one State drama group.

Professor Koch had been dreaming of the day when North Carolina communities would not only produce plays in organized groups, but would be writing their own dramas and comedies. The ground was now prepared; the State was ready.

### C.D.A. Festivals and Carolina Playmaker Tours

The declared purpose of *The Carolina Dramatic Association* was to find means of promoting and encouraging dramatic art and stimulating playwriting in North Carolina. To accomplish these ends Dr. Koch and his assistants utilized two methods: state-wide festivals and competitions, and extensive tours of Carolina Playmaker companies performing their own plays.

The method of teaching one group by showing it what another similar group has done was a favorite procedure of Professor Koch's. He used it in his playwriting class, the textbook for which was a book of plays written by former North Carolina students. The reaction of the students to this book has always been the same: "If *they* could do it, so can we!"

This method was successful in the case of school and community drama groups also. In the annual festivals, beginning in the spring of 1925, drama groups from all over the State have met and competed locally in District Festivals for the honor of appearing in the finals which are staged in Chapel Hill. In this way each group is exposed to a comparison of its work with that of other similar organizations, and the comparison has been strongly conducive to the raising of the general level of standards.

In addition to the productions of plays, demonstrations of distinctive dramatic work being done over the State, exhibits of stage models, costume designs, and scrapbooks, and lectures by authorities in various fields of theatre have been regular features of these meetings. Among the guest speakers of national importance who have addressed the Festival audiences are Professor George P. Baker, Arthur Hobson Quinn, Clifford Odets, Bernice Kelly Harris, Barrett H. Clark and many others.

At least two of the Festivals held at Chapel Hill have been of importance beyond the borders of North Carolina, the *Southern Regional Conference on the Drama* in 1928 and *Drama in the South* in 1939. To these two Regional Festivals came representatives, leaders of other drama groups from the colleges and civic groups of many Southern states, to see plays, to listen

## DRAMA IN EXTENSION

to authoritative theatre men, and to hear again and again the gospel of the "People's Theatre."

To show the people of North Carolina and other States what young apprentice playwrights can do, Professor Koch organized a total of thirty-seven tours of The Carolina Playmakers covering North Carolina systematically on an average of two to three times a year and going as far afield as Texas, Missouri, Wisconsin and New England. Traveling by car, train and private "show-bus," his touring companies played in school and civic centers in North Carolina, in New York City, at Yale University and in all the states between North Carolina and New York. In 1934 they performed at the First National Folk Festival in St. Louis before an audience of thousands. In 1936 they traveled all the way to Texas to play at the Texas Centennial Exposition in Dallas.

Dr. Koch expanded the program in the autumn of 1941 when "The Carolina Playmakers Repertory Touring Company" toured for two months in their own "show-bus" playing Paul Green's *The House of Connelly* in forty towns and cities in twelve states to an audience of 25,000. The company covered New England, New York and the Middle West, traveling 8,000 miles. The tour was sponsored and booked by The Redpath Bureau and the sixteen Carolina Playmaker actors were paid Equity wages.

With this tour The Carolina Playmakers had achieved an extension of their activities to influence thousands of people on a true professional level.

### Radio Activities

It was not until 1940 that a Radio Studio was actually organized on the campus in Chapel Hill. Professor Koch was quick to take advantage of it. "The Carolina Playmakers of the Air," directed by Earl Wynn of the Department of Dramatic Art, produced programs over various local radio stations, and a series of six plays was presented over a national network of the Mutual Broadcasting Company through WRAL in Raleigh. Such well known Playmaker authors as Paul Green, Betty Smith, James Boyd, Noel Houston and Josephina Niggli were among those to write new plays for the national network series, which extended the Playmakers far beyond their usual limits to a potential audience of several millions of people. The organization flourished for three years, until Mr. Wynn left to join the Armed Services and the Navy appropriated the radio studio's physical plant.

## PIONEERING A PEOPLE'S THEATRE

### THE ADDRESSES, READINGS AND PUBLICATIONS OF PROFESSOR FREDERICK H. KOCH

A profuse and persuasive speaker, Professor Koch spoke to thousands of people all over the country in what would undoubtedly add up to hundreds of speeches in the quarter of a century during which he directed the dramatic activities of the state of North Carolina. It is not to be wondered at that nearly all of the titles of his addresses include such words as "folk-plays" and "native drama" and "playmaking" and "people's theatre," for these were the things for which he stood. Tirelessly he applied his energies to spreading the word about a people's drama and a people's theatre whenever and wherever he was given an opportunity.

Dr. Koch wrote numerous articles and pamphlets during his active life; but important as these publications were in making his work known throughout the country, his most important literary work would seem to be the eight books of plays he edited, every one of them filled with plays his students had written. There can be little doubt that they comprise some of the most effective extension work he did. They have been a definite influence on the playwriting in this country for the last fifteen years. Judging by the annual royalty reports, some of the plays are done every year, not only in this country, but as far away as England.

An unique venture was *The Carolina Play-Book*, now in its seventeenth year of publication, and its later supplement, *The Carolina Stage*. An idealistic success, *The Carolina Play-Book* was honored with the distinction of being one of only three theatre publications included in the International Exhibit at the Century of Progress Exposition in Chicago, the other two being *Theatre Arts Monthly* and *Stage*.

As a young man at Harvard University Professor Koch earned a good deal of his keep and tuition by giving spirited Shakespeare readings. Up until the last year of his life he continued to give one-man performances of Shakespearean plays, clinging with a warm enthusiasm to the old, heroic style of acting—a style that in his hands was most effective. He had done it so often that he knew whole plays by heart, favoring *Hamlet* and *A Midsummer Night's Dream*.

In the second year of his career as a teacher at the University of North Dakota, Professor Koch read Charles Dickens' *A Christmas Carol* to a gathering of his colleagues. The reading was so successful that he was called upon to repeat it for the students and eventually for the public. This was the origin of his annual readings of this beloved ghost-story, readings that took him far and wide to great cities and small communities, goodnaturedly pushing his way through the snowy nights of winter in order to meet his many dates and leaving behind him the spirit of "The Ghost of Christmas Present." It took him to Town Hall in New York and his voice was heard over a National Radio Network for several years, reaching out all over the country with his spirited characterization of old Scrooge. In thirty-nine years these readings exceeded two hundred in number. *A Christmas Carol* came to be an institution, anticipated as a traditional high point in the yuletide by young and old in many communities, and was probably the most important work Professor Koch did. The spirit of warmth and tenderness which he left behind him on those missions of love was unforgetable.

The spirit of this energetic teacher is still stirring all through the American Theatre. Applying principles which are closely akin to those of the Abbey Theatre, he approached the dream of an American People's Theatre even as Yeats and Synge and Lady Gregory had striven for an Irish Theatre. For one who has worked with The Carolina Playmakers it is impossible to avoid making this comparison. The spirit of the Abbey Theatre Players is everpresent. But the burden which Mr. Koch lifted onto his own shoulders was possibly a greater one than that which was carried by Yeats. The latter was reaching out to the limited population of a small island with a theatre situated in a comparatively large city, the capital city of the land, sooner or later visited by almost everyone in Ireland. The Theatre of Frederick H. Koch was in a tiny village far away from the metropolitan centers. Through this small theatre it was his desire to reach millions of people in a vast land. It would have been manifestly impossible for him to carry out his plans had he concentrated all his work in Chapel Hill. His only alternatives were extension work and touring. Being a man of expansive imagination he was impelled to cultivate these fields to the utmost. However, as the territory he was trying to develop was by nature expansive, he was faced with tremendous handicaps not existing in the little Ireland of Yeats.

In Ireland it was possible to achieve a National Theatre within the span of a lifetime. In great, sprawling America it remains a goal of the future. There are indications, however, that the seed has taken root.

Of one hundred and forty plays entered in the National Playwriting Contest of the Pittsburgh Drama League last year, at least a hundred would have fallen under his denomination of American Folk Plays. When

## PIONEERING A PEOPLE'S THEATRE

Robert Porterfield of the Barter Theatre in Virginia announces that he is planning twenty-two Veterans' Theatres after the war with the hope that they will eventually grow into twenty-two people-supported State Theatres, we can be sure that "Proff" will meet him up the road somewhere, for that is an old road for him. He must have rejoiced last year when John Golden, the New York producer, contributed $100,000 toward the inauguration of a National Theatre in this country.

The men and women who were students of Professor Koch or who were touched in some way by his magic wand are not satisfied with our American Theatre. Theirs is a vision destined little by little to come true. They are aware that day by day a "people's drama" is being written, and their hope is that the end of the war will see a vigorous resumption of Frederick H. Koch's struggle for a "people's theatre" dedicated to the performance of these plays.

Here in Chapel Hill such a theatre is to be erected to the memory of this great teacher, and a higher standard of professional training for the students is being planned. Already the possibilities of much more extensive tours are being discussed; and though the body of the man who first saw the vision is dead, his spirit will be present when the final goal is reached.

## The American Theatre Today

The American theatre today is not on Broadway but in the thousands upon thousands of amateur and non-professional groups in the hamlets and towns, in the granges, the high schools, the colleges, universities, trade union halls, army posts, and in the civic centers everywhere. It is the theatre of the whole vast United States.... Where there were once five thousand theatre stages in the country and all an extension of Broadway and its syndicalists, now there are twenty-five, thirty, even fifty thousand, built and created by people themselves for their own needs, their feelings, purposes and vision. And here night after night they act and see acted and set forth in all intensity and sincerity dramas and stories of their own choosing and often of their own writing.... Here is a vast and growing theatre, rugged and dynamic in its nature, and the gloss and finish, wherever it is lacking, will ultimately be polished into being.

—Paul Green. In his *The Hawthorne Tree*.

# Presence by the River

### By Paul Green

THERE was once an old question as to who could chart the winds and the nature thereof and who could foretell the weather and its whims. The question still stands today unanswered as it did in Job's time. No doubt there are laws governing all such phenomena, and maybe someday these laws will be understood—laws that have no irrational phantom dancing within them. But even so those who understand will have no power to bring either drought or rain, for the wind will still blow where it listeth and it will rain when it will rain.

And as with the weather, so with writing a play—so with any work of art. It comes pretty much when it will come, is absent when it will be absent, and no man can provide its presence at his will. So if I may be personal in replying to your question, "Why do you write plays," I can on first consideration easily say, "I don't know." It is much like the weather to me—the what and the why, the wherefore and results. About the only answer I would venture is that I seem to need to. If I were certain that the drama were the one means of gaining honor or wealth or mental stability there would be some obvious sense in spending one's life trying to set down lines for people to speak on a stage. I believe I should want to write plays, though, if little or nothing came of them, but naturally I want a lot to come of them.

Of course your question goes further than any easy answer or any meteorological metaphor. It raises the whole problem of aptitude and calling. I think all people are by nature artists, that is, more or less so. The usual European designation of the American builder and business man as a money hog, for instance—a creature who takes pleasure only in dollar profit and pain only in dollar loss—seems to me obviously false. There is more to it than that—always more. Sinclair Lewis in one of his novels, "Work of Art," tries his hand at showing that one Myron Weagle with his dream of a perfect hotel might be considered essentially an artist. There is a lot of human truth in his contention.

## PIONEERING A PEOPLE'S THEATRE

Now if all of us have this so-called artistic urge, then why do some of us become hotel keepers and others banjo-pickers or playwrights? That is the next question. The answer is perhaps that circumstances always play their part. One child happens to have access, say, to a piano near at hand but finds his fingers too stiff or too short to allow of his becoming a performer. Perhaps he turns to composing, or bricklaying. And so it goes. Each of us could make some sort of statement as to his proper calling. Take your own case—you run a drama magazine. All sorts of odds and ends of circumstances and people went into your choice of that career.

Two incidents happened to me years ago, I remember, which turned me to writing plays. Norman Foerster, who was one of the finest English teachers ever to appear at the University of North Carolina, announced in class one day that the seniors had decided to do a play at Commencement and were holding a contest for original scripts. He advised me to try my hand. I took a chance at the thing and happened to win out. The play was produced in the forest theatre and I was thrilled to death. After that though I didn't set my heart on playwriting, for I had always been more interested in poetry and short stories than anything else. Then in 1919 "Proff" Koch came riding in from the Dakota prairies, his arms full of plays and his head full of dreams. In no time a stage was up, and everybody near and far, little and big, black and white realized for the first time that he, said body, was an artist of some sort—mainly a dramatic artist. Some went in for designing, some for acting, some for writing. I chose the last. And after a few productions, I was caught fast in my choice and had struck acquaintance with all the bat-like terrors that inhabit the shadows of the stage.

Your next question is easier to answer. "Why do you write the plays you do?" The answer is—that's the only kind I know how to write. Most of the plays I have written can be designated as folk plays, and I know this seems a narrow boundary. Perhaps it is, but since the "folk" are the people who seem to matter most to me, I have little interest in trying to deal with others who are more foreign and therefore less real to me. Not for a moment do I claim to have done justice to an inspiring subject matter, but the challenge is there, clearer, sharper, and more compelling every day. For there is something in the life of "the people" which seems of deeper significance so far as the nature of the universe goes than the characters who might be termed sophisticated. To examine the matter a little further, it seems to me that the folk are those living closer to a terrible and all-wise nature than their brethren of the sidewalks and opera house, and if I were seeking a philosophical statement for the matter it would be somewhat as follows:

The folk are the people whose manners, ethics, religious and philosophical ideals are more nearly derived from and controlled by the ways of the outside physical world (Cf. Synge's "Riders to the Sea") than by the ways and institutions of men in a specialized society (Cf. Schnitzler's "Anatol" cycle). And the outside natural world is the fountain of wisdom, the home of the fruitful all-mother, the omnipotent God. The line of demarcation between the folk and sophisticated drama is not always easily contrasted; to instance once more, Ferenc Molnar's "The Guardsman" and S. Ansky's "The Dybbuk." And between the last two I'd always choose "The Dybbuk"—even though technique should shift for itself.

I don't claim that sophisticated drama may not be great in its own right, but somehow I never thrill to it as I do to what I like to term the folk drama the Greeks wrote, the kind Shakespeare and Tolstoi and Hauptmann wrote; the kind Alexis Granowsky used to produce in Russia with its lovely burden of folk imagery, music and song. In reading "Lear," for example, I always feel a sudden lift when we come to the heath scene. There is something grand and universal in the naked relationship of the old king to the powers of nature around him.

And as characters available to art purposes, to repeat, those who live as it were with their feet in the earth and their heads bare to the storms, the lightning and the gale—those who labor with their hands wresting from cryptic nature her goods and stores of sustenance—these develop a wisdom of living which seems to me more real and beautiful than those who develop their values and ambitions from rubbing shoulders in a crowded city.

And that wisdom it is which seems important—a wisdom which is a consciousness of the great eternal Presence by which men live and move and have their being and without which they die. And if the playwrights who tell of captains and lords, kings and queens, dolls and manikins, can open up the doors of crowded buildings, cut through the filmy arras that conceals our human instincts and hopes and fears and go to the first principles of human identity—then they raise the hair on our heads too with their voice from the sacred grove of Colonus. And no longer do we think of man as sophisticated or folk, but man—man alone with his God and his destiny. And when this happens—and rare is Shakespeare, rarer than the Phoenix—then the matter is all one and listeners are all one.

## PIONEERING A PEOPLE'S THEATRE

But the present clang and confusion of wheel on iron, yelling and clamor of tickets and tellers, the secrecy of vaults and locks and braggarty monoliths of incorruptible concrete and steel—these all make it harder for us to see and hear the God who is the principle of our lives. Maybe I'm crazy on the idea of God, but then aren't we all? I refer to the wild pell mell rush every evening out of the city to the country—to the country where the birds are, where the grass is and where there is peace or should be.

Now you catch me almost carrying on into a scheme of social philosophy. And if I wanted to apply this half-surmised esthetic theory to the control and arrangement of peoples I should say there ought to be plenty of trees and land and outdoors for every man. For only in the outdoors can we associate with power and mystery in their most sublime manifestation. And heaven knows we ought to sense in any way we can whatever touch of sublimity there may be vouchsafed unto us in this darkness.

Now it seems that after all I'm saying for myself that folk-drama as such is or can be more significant than sophisticated drama. Not at all. I mean to repeat that in the last analysis it is a question of neither folk nor sophisticate—but of man, man in his environment, and it is in the main a matter for the poet, the creator, the seer. And I would say that indoors sooner or later man must perish and outdoors there is more of a chance for him.

To make another dogmatic statement, I would say that cruelty, scorn, and evils of all sorts are more native to the great cities than not, and therefore we should be better off without any great cities—I mean close, skyscraper, bedlam cities. (There's something other than politics behind Russia's efforts to create the ideal commune.) And all the little towns that get too large for their britches and so full of metropolitan urges and apings that they cut down all the trees on their main streets and cover the grass and ground with concrete will be better off when they tear up the concrete, reset the trees, and grow grass again. And maybe now that we have evolved wheels and telephones and radios and machinery of long-distance cooperation of all sorts we can all begin to live more among flowers and trees again and yet keep in touch with each other enough for our sophisticated needs. Then haply now and again we may also have a word with the Great Presence where He walks by the river bank at evening . . . .

# A Dramatic Art Building

## By Samuel Selden

FOR nineteen years The Carolina Playmakers have centered their activities in the old university building now bearing the name of The Playmakers Theatre. Erected in 1850, the building had acquired a considerable body of tradition before it was remodeled into a playhouse in 1925. In the two decades since the Playmakers entered it the old hall has added to itself a thousand more memories. They are bright memories, most of them—memories which will forever be associated with a little porticoed theatre set beside a row of green maple trees at "Carolina." For many hundreds of men and women who have come and gone—some to far-away corners of the earth—this is the beloved home and symbol of Playmaking.

Regarded from a sentimental viewpoint, the present Playmakers Theatre has taken on a certain character which could never be duplicated in any other building. It has charm, it has intimacy, it has traditions inextricably bound up with the early life of the University and with the beginnings of The Carolina Playmakers. For nineteen years, it has served well the needs of the organization housed in it. Viewed dispassionately, however, the little theatre has several unconcealable deficiencies. The activities of the Playmakers have grown so extensively in the years since their inception that the present building cannot now hold more than a small part of them. The office of the Director, the Dramatic Museum, the Business Office, the Bureau of Community Drama, the Radio Studio, the Scene Shop, the Costume Shop, and the several store rooms are located in seven different places on and off the campus—all of them outside the theatre and most of them at a considerable distance from it. The University classes in Dramatic Art have trouble finding adequate room for laboratory work, and directors are constantly hunting spots in which to hold their rehearsals.

But elbow room is not the only kind of space which is deficient in the present building. There is another, and perhaps even more important kind. That is the *sense of dramatic magnitude* — a sense which every student actor, playwright and scenic artist must appreciate before he can really master the techniques of the stage. One of the primary elements of dramatic effect is spaciousness. And this cannot be learned very well in a small room. It may be true that an experienced player can stand in a box and, by the force of his art, make the spectator *feel* distant horizons and the far-away stars; but when he is an apprentice he must have certain tangible images of space in order to understand space. Without them, he cannot learn how sensuously to stretch his muscles and extend his voice—to fill space with his presence. The stage in use now is very small. The proscenium opening is only nineteen feet wide, in contrast with a normal width of thirty or thirty-two feet. There are practically no wing space and almost no fly space. Influenced by these limitations, all dramatic action for the Playmaker stage must be scaled down. The result is often a distortion of the desired effect. Student craftsmen exposed constantly to such conditions tend in time to develop a tight, unnatural attitude toward the problems of pantomime, playwriting and scenery. If later they are assigned to work on full-size stages, they must learn much of their techniques over again.

The need for a new theatre building became apparent eight years ago. In 1936 the Playmaker staff began to lay plans. It made a careful study of the whole problem of housing Playmaker activities, and it formulated a tentative program in accordance with this study. The main divisions of the new plan were to include an Auditorium, a Stage, Scenery and Costume Shops, Dressing Rooms, Store Rooms, Class Rooms, and Offices — large enough to take care of present needs and to allow for considerable expansion in the future. Then the Playmakers looked around for an architect. They sought the advice of Donald Oenslager, Broadway designer and Professor of Design in the Yale University Department of Drama. He was largely responsible for the planning of the fine Yale Theatre. Professor Oenslager in turn consulted with Dean Meeks of the Yale School of Architecture, and the result was a recommendation of two men who were judged to be most fitted to cope with the peculiar requirements attached to the campus at Chapel Hill. The choice finally fell on Waldron Faulkner of Washington, D. C. He was approached, and he agreed immediately to undertake the designing. Several tentative plans were drawn up.

The architect and the Playmaker staff decided to consult an outside authority before they adopted a final scheme. Mr. Cleon Throckmorton, leading New York designer and consultant on many theatre projects, was turned to at this point. His reaction was clear. He advised changes in the basic articulation of the building. In the light of his experience, he said he was convinced that any scheme for a laboratory theatre should have the stage in the center, with all the other elements (School, Shops, Auditorium

## A DRAMATIC ART BUILDING

and Dressing Rooms) grouped around it in such a way as to allow one to cross from any element to another without having to pass over the Stage. This was certainly a logical idea. It seemed so utterly sound that Mr. Faulkner, already somewhat restless over the conditions hitherto imposed on him, asked if he might scrap all the older schemes and present a new one. With this permission granted, he completely redrew the theatre in accordance with Mr. Throckmorton's suggestion. This required a search for a new site, because the revised plan demanded a considerably larger area of ground than the one then assigned to it. Finally, with the help of the University Buildings and Grounds Committee, a satisfactory plot was picked in the New Campus on the level ground just east of the Bell Tower. It is a beautiful spot. Set in the edge of the University Woods and flanked by one of the paths leading to Kenan Stadium, it is just across the road from the Library. While the location is now some distance from the center of campus activities, it lies directly in the path of future expansion. With the development of the New Campus, the center of university life is bound to shift. A building erected on the site selected will then be very favorably located.

The present plans for the new Dramatic Art Building are shown in the diagrams on the following pages. The basic composition includes four wings, comprising Auditorium, School, Shops, and Dressing Rooms, grouped around the Stage in the middle. In this arrangement, the Stage becomes the pivot and radial center for all activities in the building. At the same time, means are provided for traffic between the four wings—especially between the School block and the Shops and Dressing Rooms—without a crossing on the stage. This scheme permits work in the rear and two side blocks to continue without fear of any disturbance to rehearsals and performances in progress on the stage.

A glance at the plan of the first floor shows an ample stage house with a total inside width of seventy feet, depth of thirty-eight feet, and a proscenium opening of thirty-two feet. The gridiron is sixty-five feet above the floor. The Auditorium is designed to hold slightly more than five hundred spectators. Since the University already has a large auditorium in Memorial Hall, the seating capacity for the new theatre is, perhaps, adequate. One of the leading desires of the architect and his advisers from the departmental staff is to carry over into the new theatre some of that intimacy which constitutes a principal part of the old theatre's charm. The placement of the Business Office, Lobby and Coat Rooms is conventional. A

## PIONEERING A PEOPLE'S THEATRE

cloister on each side of the Auditorium makes it possible for one to reach the Stage from the front of the house on this floor without undue exposure to the weather. The School block on the first floor contains the Green Room, the Drafting Room, and the Library. The Library is so located that it may be readily accessible to the artists in the Drafting Room, craftsmen in the School as a whole, and the technicians in the Shops. Opening off the Green Room is a small pantry for the use of actors and technical people having to work late; and near one of the outer entrances is an information booth for students and visitors.

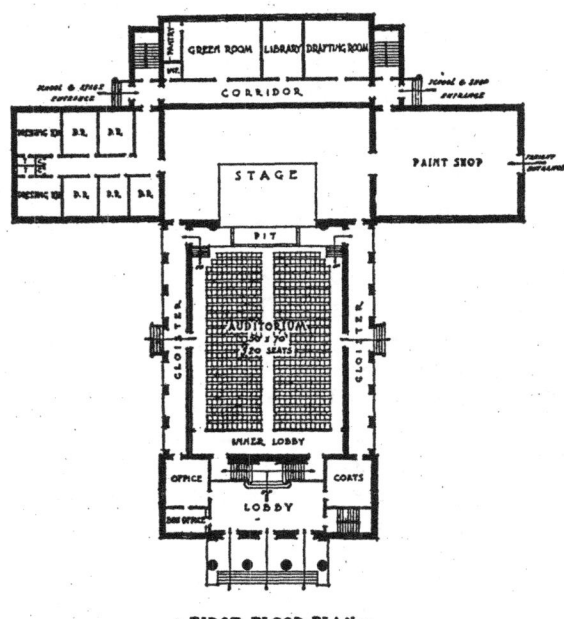

• FIRST FLOOR PLAN •

The Dressing Rooms are in a block near one School entrance, and the Scene Shops are in a block near the other. The Paint Shop is two stories high. On the floor directly below is the Construction Shop where scenery is built—out of earshot of the stage. When the units have been assembled, they may be passed up through a slot to the floor above where they will be painted. The Paint Shop, when not in use for painting, can be made to serve as an emergency dock for scenery and properties.

## A DRAMATIC ART BUILDING

If one turns to the plan of the second floor, one sees the upper parts of the Stage, Auditorium and Paint Shop. The Costume Shop where costumes will be designed, made and stored is directly over the Dressing Rooms on the floor below. The control of costume and make-up work is thus unified. Over the Lobby in the front of the house is a Museum for showing books, stage drawings, models and other materials of general interest. At one end is the Office of the Director, and at the other that of his Secretary, who will from this situation control the entrance to the Museum. On the second floor of the School block are located Office and Seminar Rooms. On the floor just above there are two more large rooms for rehearsal purposes. The balcony over the Auditorium contains a projection booth for motion-pictures.

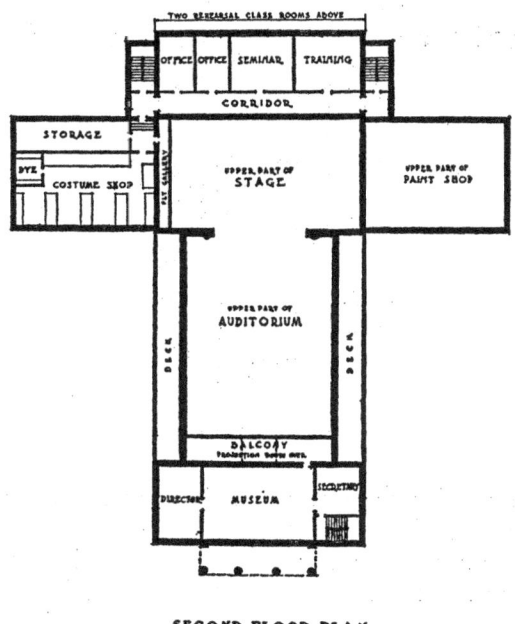

SECOND FLOOR PLAN

The basement of the building is a very busy place. Under the Lobby is a Lounge where audiences can gather during intermissions. The Lounge serves also as a lobby to the Rehearsal Theatre on this floor. This second theatre, smaller than the one on the main floor, will be used for rehearsals and for the Experimental Tryouts of new scripts. The auditorium is directly under the main Auditorium and its stage is under the trapped portion of the main Stage. Corridors on each side make it possible for one to reach the rear of the building without going out-of-doors. The rest of the basement is set aside largely for storage purposes and for supplementary Dressing Rooms.

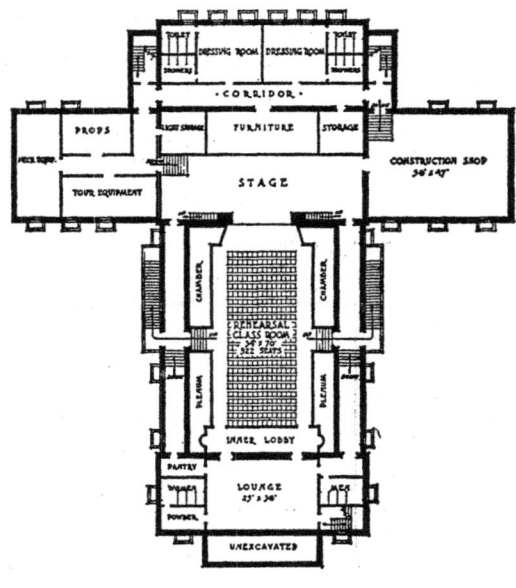

· BASEMENT PLAN ·

Since the time these drawings were made, plans have gone forward for the development of an All-University Radio Studio. Because much of the equipment and personnel which would be employed in it would have to be drawn from the theatre organization, it would seem logical for the Studio to be placed in or near the projected building here described. Several ideas have been advanced. One is to locate the Radio rooms on top of the School block. Another, and probably better, idea is to construct a separate building back of the Theatre. If some day the University should erect also, as planned, a small studio for the making of educational and dramatic films, this unit with the radio unit might together fill out a design around a little service court behind, or beside, the main playhouse.

# Miracle at Manteo

F YOU'RE looking for the birth of a communal theatre in this country, watch Roanoke Island, for here is maturing a dramatic innovation which is taking its place in the economic pattern of the community.

—Anthony F. Merrill, *The Baltimore Sunday Sun,* Oct. 9, 1938.

*The Lost Colony*, Paul Green's drama of American democracy, was presented each summer from 1937 through 1941 in the Waterside Theatre on Roanoke Island at the site of the old "Citie of Raleigh." A culmination of the annual local celebrations held since 1894, *The Lost Colony* began as a commemoration of the three hundred fiftieth anniversary of the founding of the first English colony in the New World.

The production, designed and directed by Samuel Selden, merged Manteo townspeople—business men, housewives and children—with CCC boys, professional actors, singers from the Westminster Choir School of Princeton, New Jersey, and a group of actors and technicians from The Carolina Playmakers into a homogeneous dramatic spectacle. The result was so potent dramatically that *The Lost Colony* grew quickly from a local celebration into a national institution, interrupted only by the exigencies of war.

The impact upon the nation of the uniquely American drama is evidenced in excerpts from the writings of leading critics.

—Editor's Note.

Mr. Green has written history with a compassion that turns his characters into unconscious symbols of a brave new world. He has communicated their earnestness by contrasting the egotistical court of Queen Elizabeth with the rude austerity of life inside the embattled log fort amid hostile savages. The dances translate the freshness and wildness of the new world more eloquently than words or scenery could. The glory of the ancient English hymns, carols and ballads, sung to an organ accompaniment, pulls the lost colonists into the great stream of human nobility. Part pageant, part masque, *The Lost Colony* is a simply stated idealization of the adventurous impulse that founded this nation in the restless image of Shakespeare's England. We can be wise 350 years after the event. Mr. Green's wisdom is rooted in a poet's love of a fair land. . . .

Being chiefly a community enterprise, it overflows with sincerity. For the simple things, when they are honestly intended, are both humbling and exalting. They are more religious than sermons. They are the truth of the spirit that oftentimes makes men greater than they mean to be.

—Brooks Atkinson. *The New York Times*, August 15, 1937.

---

To Paul Green and his associates, the whole Roanoke Island venture has become a broad canvas for theatrical experiment. This has been done along the most independent lines, and with no regard for what Broadway and the Schuberts would have done under similar circumstances. . . .

They shy from producing a 'pageant,' just as many audiences refuse to watch them. But in *The Lost Colony*, there are scenes in which masses of people on the wide stage make the effects. . . . An opera could be written on the Virginia Dare story, but the superb music of the Westminster Choir and an organ woven subtly into the story serves far better. . . .

All the so-called modern staging systems are used. A permanent set behind movable flats and props and two side platforms are used alternately. By clever lighting, the eleven scenes move along without a second's wait. . . . The production pleased the First Lady, Mrs. Eleanor Roosevelt, who arrived last night sitting in the back of a CCC truck with a large party. It probably will please equally the 100,000 expected to see it before the season closes. . . . Paul Green's major dramatic experiment. . . .

—John Selby, *Associated Press Arts Editor*.

---

The conventional musical show is a shabby frame for robust material; the familiar pattern of libretto, song, dance and low comedy flattens out an honest subject. What the American saga needs to arouse an audience is a serious work of art—part masque, part pageant, part symphonic drama, based conscientiously on the known facts of our history. Paul Green's *The Lost Colony*, produced during the summer at Roanoke Island, N. C., is a case in point. It was the idealized story of Sir Walter Raleigh's mysteriously tragic attempt to found a colony in America in 1587; it was written out of a profound love for our heritage, set to old English music and folk dances and staged with exalting reverence.

—Brooks Atkinson. *The New York Times*, September 12, 1937.

# Retrospect and Prospect

### By George R. Coffman

TWENTY-SIX years ago Frederick H. Koch, to use his happy phrasing, came back home again "among the red hills and green pines" of his ancestral South. With his coming, the history of The Carolina Playmakers began. With his passing August 16, 1944, its historian must turn back to 1918 and on page one write Retrospect as the chapter heading. Professor, dreamer, builder—these are the key words for that unwritten chapter. In its beginnings the scope of The Carolina Playmakers was Chapel Hill. In 1944, it embraced the Continent.

During those early years when Professor Koch and Paul Green and Elizabeth Lay, Hubert Heffner and Thomas Wolfe, and others of the playwriting group sat around "the long black walnut table" in the library, their efforts centered almost exclusively on the campus of the University. Soon Professor Koch through the annual state festival and drama tournament of the Carolina Dramatic Association broadened his activities to include all of North Carolina. The wider range came next with The Carolina Playmaker tours, extending geographically from the deep South to Washington, New York, and Boston. As Professor Koch spread far and wide the gospel of the "folk play" through lectures and summer school teaching, he became internationally known. Then, in turn, critics and historians of American drama gave him first ranking as leader of a regional movement for native drama.

It is fitting that here in Chapel Hill Professor Koch should have envisioned such a dream and should have made it a reality. The University of North Carolina is the home of dreamers, seers, and builders of a new economic and cultural South. The Nation's Problem Number One is and has been their opportunity. The briefest roll call suggests the band of choice spirits with whom Fred Koch became allied as colleague when he came from North Dakota to North Carolina. Professor E. C. Branson in 1914, under the inspiration of President Edward Kidder Graham, founded the Department of Rural Social Economics to study and develop constructive policies for the country life of this commonwealth. Its business was to teach the citizens of the state the "North Carolina of day-after-tomorrow." In 1922

## PIONEERING A PEOPLE'S THEATRE

a group of ten faculty members conceived the idea which under the directorship first of Dr. L. R. Wilson and later of Mr. W. T. Couch developed into one of the best university presses in the United States. Next in order, in 1924 Dr. Howard W. Odum became first director of the University of North Carolina Institute for Research in Social Science. The far-flung range of its activities and the dynamic energy of its director reach from studies in sociology, economics, history, geography, and law to folklore and other fields of linguistics and literary interests. Then there is Dr. J. G. deR. Hamilton, who in 1927 began to work out a project conceived several years earlier and who today knows every highway and byway of every Southern state. As a result, from public offices and private attics he has massed 2,000,000 manuscripts—the Southern Historical Collection. These manuscripts, including diaries, unpublished reminiscences, letters, plantation records, ledgers, and other documents of industrial and business undertakings form unrivaled data for a historical interpretation of practically every phase of Southern life.

So it was fitting that Dr. Greenlaw, another of these dreamers and workers, should in 1918 call Professor Koch, a new torchbearer, to the University of North Carolina. Here what he did yesterday, what his fellow-workers are doing today, and what they and others will do tomorrow are being "woven into the romance of the Southern institutions."

In this Sesquicentennial year of the University and in this volume of its publications entitled *Pioneering a People's Theatre*, it is highly fitting that we now look to the future of all that The Playmakers and its founder have come to represent. It is a nucleus and a symbol; and it is still the living embodiment of a creed. Around it a university department is to be further consolidated and developed and to be coordinated with allied departments in the creative and interpretative arts. Its leaders through The Carolina Dramatic Association should continue in the spirit of its founder to be the inspiring force and the guiding counsel for wholesome and constructive dramatic entertainment in every rural community and in every town and city of this State. The annual festival of this Association in the Koch Memorial Theatre, combined with those of music and the other arts, might prove a model for a state theatre throughout the South and over the whole country. Thus through this cultural medium a great contribution might be made to the physical and spiritual regeneration of our people as a whole.

In prospect it seems especially fitting this Sesquicentennial year to suggest a project here outlined in brief. This project would be a comprehensive history of drama in the South. Such a history would use studies that have been made or are being made, for example, of the history of dramatic production in Williamsburg and Richmond, Charleston and New Orleans. It would evaluate these and other dramatic activities down to the close of the colonial and post-colonial periods in relation to the political, social, and cultural life of the times. As a background to the renaissance of the past two decades, it would utilize materials collected by Dr. Hamilton, studies made through the Institute for Research in Social Science, or other books on the Southern scene by the University Press. Most important as basic material in the South for the past twenty-five years would be the carefully filed and documented records preserved by Professor Koch. Again, with this period of the renaissance the historian would study creation in drama in comparison with other literary activities here in the South. And finally, he would evaluate this whole movement through the South for a native drama in relation to similar movements abroad and in this country.

But, to return, the great task implicit in realizing a people's theatre—a task nobly begun—is one to which The Playmakers through the Department of Dramatic Art in the University may highly dedicate itself.

## Credo

From the first our particular interest has been the making of fresh dramatic forms, in playwriting and in acting. We have cherished the locality, believing that if the locality were interpreted faithfully, it might show us the way to the universal. For if we can see the lives of those about us with understanding—with imagination—why may we not interpret that life in significant images for all? It was so with the Greeks before us, and with our own English forebears. It has been so in all lasting art. It should be so for us here in America.

—Frederick H. Koch. *The Carolina Play-Book*, Vol. XVI, No. 1.

# The Staff of the Carolina Playmakers

#### By Marion Fitz-Simons

WHEN a theatre history is written, the historian—if he be a wise and just chronicler—emerges not with a calendar of dates and productions, although they serve as milestones, but with a group of personalities, of living men and women. The theatre idea may be one man's dream and one man's vision; but the theatre in practice and the theatre growing is a laminated structure built of the energies, shaped by the minds and colored with the imaginations of all who have worked in it and for it. So with the Playmaker Theatre and the Department of Dramatic Art which has grown up around it: the story of the people who have directed the course of the last twenty-six years is the story of the development of a college department, extended to include most of the tributary theatre arts, and a Theatre with at least state-wide impact. The Playmaker Staff, although by no means the only people who have contributed toward the design and structure of the theatre, are at least the core; and the sum of their efforts is the organization as it is known today.

George V. Denny, Carolina graduate and actor in the first Playmaker production, *When Witches Ride*, was the first staff member, becoming Business Manager of the Playmakers and Instructor of Play Production in 1924. His genius for promotion and real understanding of publicity values led him to organize the first subscription audience and to book the first tours, which carried the Playmaker name and gospel throughout North Carolina, and on up the eastern seaboard as far north as Boston. He also directed and acted in a number of productions. In 1926, he resigned to enter the professional theatre; and is now president of Town Hall in New York and founder and director of Town Hall of the Air.

P. L. Elmore, in 1923, while still a student, became Playmaker Stage Manager, which position he held after graduation in 1925 until his resignation in 1927 to enter the professional theatre. Lee Elmore has been in and out of the theatre since leaving the Playmakers, alternating directing (most recently of *The Day Will Come* for Leo Birinski) with his position as an official of Lord and Taylor department store in New York.

## THE STAFF OF THE CAROLINA PLAYMAKERS

Hubert C. Heffner, himself a Playmaker actor and author of *Dod Gast Ye Both*, joined the staff in 1926, after having taught at the University of Wyoming and the University of Arizona. He was Assistant Director and headed the Playmaker work in the year 1926-27, when Professor Koch was away on leave. Under his very successful management, Playmaker touring became not only an established institution, but such a lucrative one that it almost entirely financed the Chapel Hill productions of the Playmakers. He is author, with Samuel Selden and Hunton D. Sellman, of *Modern Theatre Practice*. He left in 1930 to head the dramatic work at Northwestern University, where he stayed until called in 1938 to be head of the Department of Speech and Drama at Stanford University, which post he still holds.

\*Samuel Selden came in 1927 as Instructor in Dramatic Art and first Technical Director of the Playmakers. A graduate of Yale, professional actor, stage manager, and technical director—listing experience with The Provincetown Playhouse, the Theatre Guild, the Intimate Opera Company, the road company of Eugene O'Neill's *Desire Under the Elms*, and five resident and traveling stock companies—he offered courses in the Construction and Painting of Scenery, Stage Lighting, Acting and Directing. Under his tutelage the theatre techniques of the Playmakers definitely emerged from the pioneer period. In 1929 he went on leave from the University to the New York School of Fine and Applied Art to study Art and Architecture; in 1930 he became Assistant Professor of Dramatic Art and Assistant Director of Playmakers; in the summers of 1932 and 1933 he studied at Columbia University in New York; in 1937 he directed Paul Green's *The Lost Colony*, which ran for five succeeding summers until closed in 1941 by wartime restrictions; in 1938 he was awarded a Guggenheim Fellowship and spent half the year in New York in study and the other half in touring the theatres of Europe; in the same year he became Associate Professor of Dramatic Art and Associate Director of the Playmakers. During these years, he worked insistently on the curriculum of the Dramatic Art Department, initiating new courses both on the undergraduate and graduate levels, teaching a wide range of technical courses, and assisting with the teaching of Professor Koch's courses in Playwriting. Through this period, he was also writing a number of books, at least two of which lead popularity lists of

---

⁋ \* The asterisk is used here and hereinafter to indicate that the person is a member of the present staff of The Carolina Playmakers.

theatre texts for colleges and high schools. *Stage Scenery and Lighting*, a collaboration with Hunton D. Sellman, *A Player's Handbook, Modern Theatre Practice*, with sections by Hubert Heffner and Hunton Sellman, and *The Stage in Action* are to be joined this year by a new actor's text, soon to be published by F. S. Crofts. Since the death of Professor Koch in the summer of 1944, Mr. Selden has been Acting Head of the Department of Dramatic Art and Director of the Playmakers.

ELMER HALL, a graduate of Massachusetts Normal Art School, has been associated with the Playmakers on several separate occasions, the first of these being in 1929-30 when Samuel Selden was on leave in New York. In 1929 and again in the summer of 1931, Elmer Hall was temporary Technical Director and Instructor in theatre techniques. In 1938 he again joined the staff as Assistant Professor of Dramatic Art and Technical Director of Playmakers, giving courses in Scene Design, Construction, and Painting and Stage Lighting. His chief contribution to the body of Playmaker tradition was a healthy respect for fine craftsmanship. He left in 1940 to become head of the drama work at McGill University in Canada.

RALPH WESTERMAN came from the Cape Playhouse in Dennis, Massachusetts, where he had been a staff member for a number of years, to become Business Manager for the year 1930-31. Mr. Westerman left to go to the west coast to take a position in extension work in adult education.

†HARRY E. DAVIS came to the Playmakers in 1931, after having taught at Mississippi State College for Women and having been for two years director of the Town Theatre and the Children's Theatre in Columbia, South Carolina. He became Technical Director and Business Manager of the Playmakers and Instructor in Dramatic Art, teaching courses in Scene Design and Construction and Stage Lighting. In 1933 he organized the Junior Carolina Playmakers, a children's group which presented plays for a child audience. Two of these, *Ali Baba and the Forty Thieves* and *Cinderella* were also written by Mr. Davis. In 1937 he organized, directed and acted with a group, selected from and sponsored by The Carolina Playmakers, which presented a summer season of Carolina plays at the Nantucket Yacht Club, Nantucket, Massachusetts. In the same year he was relieved of the duties of Business Manager and became an Assistant Professor of Dramatic

---

† This symbol is used here and hereinafter to designate members of the Playmaker Staff on leave with the Armed Services.

## THE STAFF OF THE CAROLINA PLAYMAKERS

Art and Assistant Director of Playmakers. In the summer of 1939, he became Stage Manager of *The Lost Colony* and played the part of the First Soldier, and was Associate Director of that play in 1939 and 1940. He went on leave to Columbia University for further study in the fall of 1939, returning in 1940 to hold his position of Technical Director. In the fall of 1941, he managed the Playmaker company of *The House of Connelly* on an extensive Redpath Tour and played the part of "Robert Connelly." He left in 1942 to join the army.

ORA MAE DAVIS, wife of Harry Davis and "Mammy" to several generations of Playmakers, came in 1931 to find the costume department practically not extant, except for the volunteer services of faculty wives, notably Mrs. Prouty and Mrs. Valentine. At first her field by a sort of default, Playmaker costuming later became her own province by divine right of indefatigable labor and fearless undertaking of staggering assignments which piled Shakespearean productions on top of operettas and climaxed the whole by the brilliant dressing of the two Paul Green symphonic dramas, *The Lost Colony* and *The Highland Call*. At the time of her death in the spring of 1942, costuming had been raised, solely through her efforts, to a major technical department of Playmakers and to a place in the college curriculum. Mrs. Davis also gave work in dance and body training, though always on an extra-curricular basis, and designed the movement for several of the operettas and Shakespearean productions.

PHOEBE BARR, ex-Denishawn dancer, came to Chapel Hill in 1931; and although she was never officially a member of the Playmaker Staff, the impact of her work upon Playmaker activities is still apparent. In the fall of 1932 she organized a private dance group of men and women. At the same time she associated herself with the Playmakers as an actor, as visiting lecturer on movement for the stage, and choreographer for the outdoor productions and operettas. The performance in Kenan Stadium in the summer of 1932 of *Alcestis*, with choric dances created by Mrs. Barr, fully demonstrated the compelling power of the integration of music, dance, and drama; and since that year, no outdoor production, no operetta has been presented by The Carolina Playmakers without dancing designed to decorate and amplify it. Mrs. Barr's stimulation of individual students is apparent from the record: six professional dancers and teachers of dance list her as first teacher; and many more actors, teachers, writers, students in widely divergent fields were influenced to the profound benefit of themselves and their work.  Mrs. Barr left Chapel Hill in 1936, when her husband was called to the faculty of Tulane University.

DARICE PARKER, departmental secretary-extraordinary from 1934, and as such, ex-officio staff member, took over the duties of Business Manager and Executive Secretary of the Carolina Dramatic Association when her husband, John Parker, left to join the army in 1942. A storehouse of information, master diplomat and wise to the delicate adjustments necessary between the sprawling, ramified elements of so complex an organization, she was sorely missed when, in the summer of 1943, she resigned to be with her husband.  She was active for a season in U. S. O. work.

*PAUL GREEN joined the Playmaker Staff officially in 1936. Member of the early illustrious group of pioneer Playmakers, philosopher, poet, essayist, novelist, scenarist, author of *In Abraham's Bosom* (Pulitzer Prize Play in 1927), *The House of Connelly* (produced in New York in 1931), *Johnny Johnson* (Broadway production in 1936), *The Lost Colony* (presented at Fort Raleigh on Roanoke Island 1937-1941), *The Highland Call* (given in Fayetteville in 1939 and 1940), *Native Son* (a dramatization of the novel by Richard Wright produced in New York in 1941), *Shroud My Body Down, Enchanted Maze, The Field God, Roll Sweet Chariot, The Man Who Died at Twelve O'Clock, The No 'Count Boy*, and other plays, many of which had their first production in the Playmaker Theatre — he became literary adviser to the Playmakers and Professor of Dramatic Art, teaching seminars in Philosophical Ideas in Dramatic Art, and Technical Problems in Playwriting in the newly formed graduate division of the Dramatic Art Department. He apportions his time now between Chapel Hill and Hollywood, following his own profession on the one hand and guiding the professional skills of the students on the other.

HOWARD W. BAILEY, one-time Playmaker, later actor and radio actor in New York and elsewhere, then North Carolina Director of Federal Theatre Projects, became in 1937 Business Manager of the Playmakers and first Instructor of Voice and Diction in the Dramatic Art Department. Throughout the five summers of *The Lost Colony*, he played the part of "Lord Essex," and in 1941 became Associate Director of the play. Mr. Bailey stayed with the Staff only one year, leaving to become director of drama at Rollins College in Florida.

†JOHN W. PARKER, former Playmaker, author of *Sleep on, Lemuel*, and

## THE STAFF OF THE CAROLINA PLAYMAKERS

State Director of the Bureau of Community Drama from 1934, became Business Manager of the Playmakers in 1938. As Executive Secretary of the Carolina Dramatic Association, he traveled extensively over the state, helping to organize groups, giving extension courses in theatre work and helping to direct plays. He directed several pageants, and is perhaps best known in the state for staging and directing *The Highland Call*, by Paul Green, in Fayetteville in 1939 and 1940. Mr. Parker made a lasting contribution to the cause of drama in the State in his work with the organization of dramatic curricula in the high schools. He has been on leave since 1942, serving with the U. S. Army.

†EARL WYNN came to the Playmakers in 1938 from Northwestern University to become Instructor in Voice and Diction and to organize courses in Radio Acting and Production. In 1939 he directed the radio productions of "The Carolina Playmakers of the Air" with programs at first for a local, then a state, and finally a national audience. In the summers of 1940 and 1941 he played "Governor White" in *The Lost Colony*. Mr. Wynn resigned in 1942 to work as a civilian with the Quartermaster Corps of the U. S. Army and has since joined the Navy and is now in Hollywood writing scripts for Naval training films.

†LYNN GAULT, one-time Playmaker, became the first Staff Designer in 1940 when he left his position at Hiram College to join The Carolina Playmakers. A writer, author of *His Boon Companions* published in *American Folk Plays*, authority on English Folk Dance, he assisted with the scenery, directed the country dance, and, in 1941, played the "Master of Ceremonies" in *The Lost Colony*. Mr. Gault remained with the Playmakers until called to enter the Army in 1942.

*IRENE SMART, who assisted in the costume work for *The Lost Colony* and *The Highland Call*, and with Playmaker costuming from 1939 to the death of Mrs. Davis, became in 1942 Director of Costumes and Assistant in the course in Costuming in the Dramatic Art Department. She has maintained the dressing of Playmaker productions on the high level established by Mrs. Davis, and given her students, in addition to a fine feeling for color and line, sound training in the fundamentals of clothing construction. She is now a full Instructor on the University faculty. In the summer of 1944, Mrs. Smart worked in New York with Eaves Costumes and later with Paul Dupont, assisting with the costuming for the productions of *Anna Lucasta* and *The Seven Lively Arts*.

## PIONEERING A PEOPLE'S THEATRE

JOSEPHINA NIGGLI, former Playmaker, Texan-Mexican playwright, author of a popular volume of one-act Mexican folk plays as well as several full-length dramas, returned to the Playmakers first as an Assistant and later, in 1942, as Instructor in the radio division. Herself an actor and playwright, her energies were more directed to script-writing and dramatic production than to technical radio. Miss Niggli resigned in 1943 and returned to her home in San Antonio, where she is at present working. Her novel, *Mexican Village*, is soon to be published by the University of North Carolina Press.

*DOUGLAS HUME, ex-Playmaker, student of Maria Ouspenskaya, actor and part-time director of The First Theatre in Monterey, California, left his position at Chico College and joined the staff in 1942 as Assistant Professor of Speech and assistant to Professor Koch in the dramatic literature courses. In 1943 he became an Assistant Professor of Dramatic Art; and in the years of the wartime manpower shortage, has doubled in brass as an extremely conscientious teacher on the one hand and an able and versatile actor on the other.

*FOSTER FITZ-SIMONS, former Playmaker, internationally known dancer, who has appeared with Ted Shawn's Men's Group one-night-standing in all of the forty-eight states, in Canada, Cuba, and England, and who, with Miriam Winslow, toured the United States and Argentina, author of *Four on a Heath*, (published in 1934 by Row, Peterson) and *Road into the Sun* (brought out in 1939 by the Dramatic Publishing Company)—became in 1942 Staff Designer and Instructor in Scene Design and Costume Design, and assistant to Professor Selden in the course in acting. In 1943 he collaborated with Tom Avera on *The Twilight Zone*, a full-length play produced as the major original of the year. For the Extension Division he has taught the course in Modern Drama, and is now reorganizing and will teach the course in Playwriting. He has served the Playmakers, in addition to his specific function of designer, as director, actor, choreographer and composer.

*ROBERT BARKER BURROWS came to the Playmakers from the position of Director of Drama in Lincoln High School, Seattle, Washington, after the beginning of the 1942 season. He has taught courses in Scene Construction and Stage Lighting, and designed the setting for the Playmaker production of *Watch on the Rhine* in 1943. In the summer of 1943 he attended Northwestern University for further study; and in the summer of 1944 he acted as technical director for the University Theatre at Ann Arbor, Michigan.

## THE STAFF OF THE CAROLINA PLAYMAKERS

Joseph Salek, ex-Playmaker, joined the Staff as Business Manager and Executive Secretary of the Bureau of Community Drama for the year 1943-44. In that year he also assisted Professor Selden in the course in acting, directed the operetta, acted in several major productions and assisted with the painting of scenery. He is now in Santa Fe, New Mexico, painting.

*Lucile Culbert became a member of the Staff in 1943 while still a graduate student in the Dramatic Art Department. She assumed the duties of Instructor in the radio branch upon Josephina Niggli's resignation; and has with consummate determination and energy achieved a new studio (the Navy having taken over the space occupied by the original one) under wartime labor conditions and, in spite of an apparently impossible wall of priorities and governmental red tape, managed to secure reasonably adequate equipment. In 1945, in conjunction with the Department of Journalism, she has been producing a series of sustaining programs through stations WPTF and WRAL in Raleigh.

*Kai Heiberg-Jurgensen, a native of Denmark, first became a Playmaker—after work with the University Theatre in Copenhagen—when he was granted a Rockefeller Assistantship in the Department of Dramatic Art in 1941. In 1942 he collaborated with Robert Schenkkan on a new translation of Ibsen's *Peer Gynt* for production in the Forest Theatre; and in 1943 his *Down to the Sea*, a full-length play, was produced by the Playmakers. In the year 1943-44 he held the position of Visiting Lecturer in Playwriting and Theatre Literature at Carnegie Institute of Technology; and in 1944 he returned, as Visiting Lecturer, to the faculty of the Carolina Dramatic Art Department. He assists Professor Selden in the Playwriting and Acting courses, edits the monthly News Letter to Playmakers in the Armed Services, and has recently helped to organize the showing of a series of fine foreign films in the Playmaker Theatre.

*Lynette Warren, who was in 1943 the able and efficient secretary in the Playmaker business office, became the Business Manager of The Carolina Playmakers, Secretary of the Bureau of Community Drama, and Executive Secretary of the Carolina Dramatic Association in 1944.

These men and women, with the single exception of Phoebe Barr, have been the paid, official members of the Playmaker Staff from the beginnings of the organization—and still the picture is not complete. The time, sympathetic interest, and encouragement of a host of other people, especially in the early difficult days, have gone into the building of this institution: members of other departments in the University—Edwin Greenlaw, Archibald Henderson, George McKie, Urban Tignor Holmes, John Manning Booker, George Coffman, Robert Sharpe, and Russell Smith, to list a few of the many—faculty wives and townspeople, Mrs. A. A. Kluttz, Mrs. Ruth Valentine, Mrs. W. F. Prouty, Mrs. U. T. Holmes, Mrs. Irene Fussler, Josephine Sharkey, Mr. and Mrs. William Meade Prince and Walter Preston among others—and the long, unsung list of graduate assistants in the Dramatic Art Department, who have given of their creative resources and have oftentimes carried responsibilities almost equal to those of the formal staff.

The mere listing of this group of people and their personal achievements is no more than a catalogue; the sum of their lives and the dedication of their energies bears potent testimony to the integrity of the theatre ideal.

## The Dramatic South

The South remains what it is—mainly a rural region whose ideologies and ethics of living are derived from the fields, the trees and the hills—a region of violent contradictions like nature itself, of startling beauty and blinding ugliness, of hate and love, of wealth and degraded poverty, of fertile land and eroded land, of bountiful rainfall and parching drought, of passion and sloth, of soaring ambition and empty death. . . . But no matter what happens, whether the ragged sharecropper winds up with hardwood floors, frigidaires, a perennial cow, electric lights, and gold teeth from the dentist or not, human drama will go on. For there is no solution to life except death. And the only mysterious thing about the South is that it is so full of both. I don't know why this is so. Only those who understand the will of God and the principles of history can explain it. For me it is enough in the main to say that the materials of songs, poems, stories, art, novels, and drama will remain here as long as men remain, in whatever condition of servitude or pride.

—Paul Green in his *Out of the South*.

# Plays Produced by the Carolina Playmakers 1918-1944

### ORIGINAL ONE-ACT PLAYS

#### 1919-1920

*When Witches Ride*, a play of folk superstition, by Elizabeth A. Lay.
*The Return of Buck Gavin*, a tragedy of a mountain outlaw, by Thomas Wolfe.
*What Will Barbara Say?*, a romance of Chapel Hill, by Minnie Shepherd Sparrow.
*Peggy*, a tragedy of a tenant farmer, by Harold Williamson.
*The Fighting Corporal*, a Negro comedy, by Louisa Reid.
*Who Pays?*, a tragedy of industrial conflict, by Minnie Shepherd Sparrow.
*The Third Night*, a ghost play of the Carolina mountains, by Thomas Wolfe.
*The Hag*, a comedy of folk superstition, by Elizabeth A. Lay.

#### 1920-1921

*Off Nag's Head*, a tragedy of the Carolina Coast, by Dougald MacMillan.
*The Last of the Lowries*, a play of the Croatan outlaws, by Paul Green.
*The Miser*, a farm tragedy, by Paul Green.
*The Vamp*, a comedy of university life, by William Royal.
*The Old Man of Edenton*, a melodrama of colonial Carolina, by Paul Green.
*The Chatham Rabbit*, a comedy of college life, by Legette Blythe.
*The Reaping*, a play of social problems, by John Terry.
*In Dixon's Kitchen*, a comedy of a country courting, by Wilbur Stout.

#### 1921-1922

*Reward Offered*, a comedy of mountain characters, by Jane Toy.
*Trista*, a play of colonial superstition, by Elizabeth A. Lay.
*Waffles for Breakfast*, a comedy of newly-married life, by Mary Yellott.
*The Lord's Will*, a tragedy of a country preacher, by Paul Green.
*Dogwood Bushes*, a romance of the Carolina country, by Wilbur Stout.
*Blackbeard, Pirate of the Carolina Coast*, by Paul Green and Elizabeth A. Lay.

#### 1922-1923

*Wrack P'int*, a melodrama of the Carolina coast, by Paul Green.
*Agatha*, a romance of the old South, by Jane Toy.
*Wilbur's Cousin*, a comedy of college life, by Ernest Thompson.
*John Lane's Wife*, a tragedy of the farm, by Mack Gorham.
*The Berry Pickers*, a Colorado folk comedy, by Russell Potter.
*Mamma*, a comedy of modern manners, by Ernest Thompson.

#### 1923-1924

*The Black Rooster*, a comedy of country folk, by Pearl Setzer.
*Nat Macon's Game*, a romance of a revolutionary patriot, by Osler Bailey.
*Gaius and Gaius, Jr.*, a comedy of plantation days, by Lucy M. Cobb.
*Servants of God*, a play of a small-town preacher, by Robert S. Pickens.
*The Beaded Buckle*, a comedy of present-day aristocracy, by Frances Gray.
*Fixin's*, a tragedy of a tenant farm woman, by Erma and Paul Green.

## PIONEERING A PEOPLE'S THEATRE

*The Younger*, a comedy of the present-day flapper, by Sue Byrd Thompson.

*The Wheel*, the evolution of a college boy, by Ernest Thompson.

### 1924-1925

*The Honor of Bonava*, a chapter from Reconstruction days, by Robert Watson Winston.

*Politicin' in Horse Cove*, a comedy of mountain folk, by Martha Boswell.

*The Scuffletown Outlaws*, a tragedy of the Lowrie gang, by William Norment Cox.

*Out of the Past*, a romance of college life at Carolina in '61, by Frances Gray.

*Yon Side O' Sunk Creek*, a tragedy of mountain folk, by Martha Boswell.

*Quare Medicine*, a country comedy of a quack doctor, by Paul Green.

### 1925-1926

*A Carolina Pierrot*, a play of Pierrot on the university campus, by William J. Macmillan.

*Clay*, a play of the farm, by David Reid Hodgin.

### 1926-1927

*Lighted Candles*, a tragedy of the Carolina Highlands, by Margaret Bland.

*The Muse and the Movies*, a comedy of Greenwich Village, by Alice Rodewald.

*Mr. Perry Writes a Play*, a burlesque of folk play writing, by William DeCatur Perry.

*The Marvelous Romance of Wen Chun-Chin*, a Chinese folk play, by Cheng-Chin Hsiung.

### 1927-1928

*Mountain Music*, a California folk play, by Edith Daseking.

*Job's Kinfolks*, a tragedy of the mill people, by Loretto Carroll Bailey.

*The Queen Has Her Face Lifted*, a fantastic satire, by Alvin M. Kahn.

*The New Eve*, an expressionistic play of the future, by Mary Dirnberger.

*Day's End*, a California folk play, by Alice Pieratt.

*A Shot Gun Splicin'*, a mountain comedy, by Gertrude Wilson Coffin.

### 1928-1929

*The Family*, an episode of the American home, by Catherine Wilson Nolen.

*Graveyard Shift*, a play of California factory workers, by Edith Daseking.

*O Promise Me*, a modern romance cycle, by Curtis Benjamin.

*The Lie*, a play of Revolutionary Carolina, by Wilkeson O'Connell.

*Black Water*, a sequel to *Job's Kinfolks*, by Loretto Carroll Bailey.

*Companion-Mate Maggie*, a Negro comedy, by Helen Dortch.

### 1929-1930

*The No 'Count Boy*, a comedy of Negro life, by Paul Green.

*Magnolia's Man*, a comedy of the mountain people, by Gertrude Wilson Coffin.

*Being Married*, a domestic comedy, by Catherine Wilson Nolen.

*For Auntie's Sake*, a comedy of college life, by John Patric.

*Hollyhocks*, a play of New England village folk, by Joseph Philip Fox.

*Suspended Animation*, a comedy of playmaking, by Kent Creuser.

*Death Valley Scotty*, a play of the California desert, by James Milton Wood.

### 1930-1931

*Samuel Hinkle, Fireman*, a comedy of New England village life, by Joseph Philip Fox.

*Cloey*, a play of Winston-Salem folk, by Loretto Carroll Bailey.

*Git Up An' Bar the Door*, a farce of Mississippi folk life, by Arthur Palmer Hudson.

*Ever' Snitch*, a comedy of Carolina fisherfolk, by Irene Fussler.

*The Blue Remembered Hills*, a play of college life, by Theodore Herman.

# PLAYS PRODUCED BY THE PLAYMAKERS, 1918-1944

*A Very Pale Pink Angel*, a whimsical satire, by Ellen Stewart.

*Always A Bettin' Man*, a comedy of Maryland folk, by Tom Loy.

## 1931-1932

*A Vision of Eugenics*, a very modern extravaganza, by Maurice Ferber.

*Old Aus Ramsey*, a comedy of Carolina mountain folk, by Charles Elledge.

*The Mandarin Coat*, a very foolish comedy, by Olive Newell.

*Those Children*, a modern comedy, by Osmond Molarsky.

*Whispering Shadows*, a tragedy of the blind, by Vernon B. Crook.

*Patches*, a comedy of family life, by Jo Norwood.

*The Last Two Shots*, a mountain tragedy, by Irene Fussler.

*Treasures*, by Irene Fussler.

*King, Queen, and Joker*, a drama of royalty, by Irene Fussler.

*Birds of a Feather*, a domestic comedy, by Jo Norwood.

*Granny*, a domestic tragedy, by Jack Riley.

*The Golden Lioness*, a fantasy of Paris in 1750, by Reuben Young Ellison.

*Proof*, a play about love, by Osmond Molarsky.

*Boardin' Out*, a mountain folk comedy, by Charles Elledge.

*Sleep On, Lemuel*, a Carolina Negro comedy, by John W. Parker.

*Bloomers*, a comedy of family life, by Jo Norwood.

*The Common Gift*, a tragedy of working women, by Elwyn de Graffenreid.

*The Loyal Venture*, a drama of colonial Carolina, by Wilkeson O'Connell.

*Neighbors of the Dead*, a tragedy of heredity (first act of a full-length play), by Vernon Crook.

*Ol' Honeycutt's Boy*, a play about a country boy, by Jack Riley.

*The Boss of the House*, a Carolina country comedy, by Lubin Leggette.

*Chicken Money*, a play of Iowa farm life, by Winifred Tuttle.

*The Battle of Shaw's Mill*, a Carolina country comedy, by Charles Elledge and Malcolm Seawell.

*Election Returns*, a social tragedy (Act I of a full-length play), by Alonzo Hoyle.

*Freights*, a drama of the side-lines, by Marjorie Craig.

*A Revolt in the Nineties*, a romance, by Anne Wilson.

*Playing With Fire*, a tragedy of country life, by Thea W. Whitefield.

*A Little Cajun*, a play of Louisiana folk, by Peg Williamson.

*It's Just Too Bad*, a tragedy of college youth, by James Alfred Stanley.

*Blessed Assurance*, a Carolina country comedy, by Evelyn McCall.

## 1932-1933

*Old Ninety-Seven*, a tragedy of railroad life, by Wilbur Dorsett.

*Nothing Ever Happens*, a modern domestic tragi-comedy, by Elmer R. Oettinger, Jr.

*Gateway*, an interlude, by Eugenia Rawls.

*Four on a Heath*, a grotesque, by Foster Fitz-Simons.

*Sour Fodder*, a play of Iowa small-town folk, by Burdette Kindig.

*Creek Swamp Nigger*, a Carolina Negro tragedy, by Harry W. Coble.

*Hell Bent for Honolulu*, a college comedy, by William Bonyun.

*And They Lived Happily*, a domestic comedy, by Marion Tatum.

*Stumbling in Dreams*, a comedy of Tin Pan Alley, by George Brown.

*Davy Crockett*, a play of the frontier, by John Philip Milhous.

*Coal*, a play of West Virginia mine folk, by Marguerite McGinnis.

*The State Rests*, a play of a small-town court, by Peggy Ann Harris.

*In His Hand*, a play of village folk, by Betty Bolton.

## PIONEERING A PEOPLE'S THEATRE

*The Elders Play*, a problem play of youth, by Sue Roberson.
*Honora Wade*, a play of Georgia folk, by Eugenia Rawls.
*Back Door*, a Carolina folk comedy, by Wilbur Dorsett.
*Fool's Justice*, a Negro tragedy, by Harry W. Coble.
*A Little Boat to India*, a springtime farce, by Foster Fitz-Simons.
*Heart Trouble*, a comedy of Georgia village folk, by Bradford White.
*Mumsey*, a drama of Long Island folk, by Sarah M. W. Huntley.
*One Every Minute*, a modern comedy, by Everett Jess.
*Malone*, an Irish folk tragedy, by Marion Tatum.
*The Last Skirmish*, a play of West Virginia mountain people, by Marguerite McGinnis.
*Second Edition*, a psychological drama, by Robert W. Barnett.
*Lights in the Sky*, an American comedy, by William Bonyun.
*Design for Justice*, a social commentary, by Elmer R. Oettinger, Jr.
*Comedy at Five*, an American comedy, by Martha Matthews Hatton.
*Mihalusek's Wager*, a drama of Polish military life, by Edward V. Conrad.
*Discontent*, a play of industrial strife, by J. M. Ledbetter, Jr.
*Blow Me Down*, a comedy of sailor folk, by William Bonyun.
*And the Poet Laughed*, a modern comedy drama, by Burdette Kindig.
*Etowah Plantation*, a legend of the land, 1846-1864, by Eugenia Rawls.
*Tintagil*, a dream play, by Martha Matthews Hatton.
*Farewell to Glamour*, a modern American comedy, by James P. McConnaughey.
*My Son*, a tragedy of a Southwest trapper, by Frank McIntosh.

*The Salted Pup*, a comedy of the time of sap and smalle fooles, by John Philip Milhous.
*The Moon Turns*, the conclusion of a youthful romance, by Elmer R. Oettinger, Jr.
*Beer on Ice*, the burp of a nation, by Harry W. Coble.
*Bull Session*, an ironic comedy of college life, by George Brown.
*For Poland*, a tragedy of the Great War, by Ed Conrad.
*No Word from the Wise*, a comedy of small-town people, by Wilbur Dorsett.
*A Mocking-Bird Singing*, a romance of the South, by Foster Fitz-Simons.
*Judgment Comes to Dan'l*, a folk comedy of eastern North Carolina, by Bernice Kelly Harris.
*Eternal Spring*, a tragedy of prejudice, by Robert Barnett.
*The Queen Was in the Kitchen*, a persistent comedy, by Ellen Stewart.
*Burgundy for Breakfast*, an effervescent farce, by Martha Matthews Hatton.
*Three Muggy Rooms in the Bronx*, a play of father and son, by George Brown.
*Henna Rinse*, a play of "Ye Venus Beauty Shoppe," by Marion Tatum.

### 1933-1934

*Showing at Eight*, a play of a small-town moving picture theatre, by Leonard Rapport.
*O Woman*, a modern comedy of an ancient tragedy, by Carl G. Thompson.
*November Night*, a play of a Pennsylvania mining town, by Margaret Belle McCauley.
*Hell's Dreams*, a play of modern life, by Frederica Frederick.
*Diana*, a moonlight chase, by Kathleen Krahenbuhl.
*Shadows of Industry*, a drama of the financial world, by Vermont C. Royster.
*Sing Your Own Song*, a comedy—we hope!, by Nat Farnworth.
*Flight Unending*, a tragedy of youth, by Robert W. Barnett.

## PLAYS PRODUCED BY THE PLAYMAKERS, 1918-1944

*Everglades and Hickory,* an episode in the life of Andrew Jackson, by John F. Alexander.
*Grand Slam,* a satiric comedy, by James Thompson.
*Copper Penny,* a modern domestic drama, by Douglas Hume.
*Bought with the Vittles,* a dude ranch comedy, by Alton Williams.
*Opposite Poles,* a play of the divorce problem, by Margaret Siceloff.
*New Rasthenia,* a nervous break-down, by Herman Fussler.
*The Head-Ax of Ingfell,* a tragedy of the Igorote hill folk of the Philippines, by Anne B. Walters.
*Driftwood,* a tragedy of the fisherfolk of eastern Carolina, by Patricia McMullan.
*La Capilla,* (The Chapel), a legendary romance of Spanish California, by Frederica Frederick.
*Over the Doorsill,* a play of small-town life, by Harry W. Coble.
*Another Journey,* a modern tragedy, by Virgil Lee.
*Borrowed of the Night,* a tragedy of youth, by Kathleen Krahenbuhl.
*Moon in the Hawthorne Tree,* a Georgia farm tragedy, by Foster Fitz-Simons.
*Prelude,* a story of youth, by Vermont C. Royster.
*The Stars Are Fire,* a comedy of earnest youth, by Nat Farnworth.
*John Brown,* an episode in his campaign in "Bleeding Kansas," by John F. Alexander.
*Oh, Hell,* a very modern political satire, by Margaret McCauley.
*Shipmates,* a play of the water-front, by Donald Pope.
*Cottie Mourns,* a comedy of sea island folk, by Patricia McMullan.
*Tomorrow,* a play of a lodging-house, by Douglas Hume.
*The Lo Fan Joss,* a subtle thing, by Herman Fussler.
*Pretty, Plump Angel,* a play of youth, by Leonard Rapport.
*Never a Second Time,* a romantic interlude, by Leonard Rapport.
*Release,* a play of courage, by Jean Smith Cantrell.
*Third Verse,* a comedy of a small-town newspaper, by Wilbur Dorsett.
*Unto the Hills,* a play of faiths, by Leonard Rapport.
*Strange Interlaken,* a vignette, by Robert Barnett.
*Lifeguards and Fish,* a modern comedy of errors, by Margaret Siceloff.
*Back Page,* a newspaper melodrama, by Don Shoemaker.
*The Golden Wedding,* a romantic comedy, by Alton Williams.
*Rich Man! Poor Man!,* a Marxian romance, by Cecilia Allen.
*When Floosies Meet,* a comedy of pseudo-artists, by Walter Terry.
*The Suicide,* a modern interpretation of hell, by Sara Seawell.
*A Beating of Wings,* a poetic tragedy, by Foster Fitz-Simons.
*Beginners,* a belligerent satire, by Bradford White.
*Belle,* a small-town tragedy, by Patricia McMullan.
*When Doctors Fail,* a comedy of faith healing, by W. A. Sigmon.
*The Skeleton Rattles His Bones,* a modern domestic comedy drama, by Douglas Hume.
*Spare-Ribs,* a comedy of nautical cookery, by Donald Pope.
*Crash,* a story of "The Street," by Milton Kalb.

### 1934-1935

*Sea Psalm,* a tragedy of Carolina sea-folk, by Charles Edward Eaton.
*New Anarchy,* a play of the banking crisis, by Philip Goddard Parker.

# PIONEERING A PEOPLE'S THEATRE

*New Nigger*, a tragedy of the tobacco country, by Fred Howard.

*Clam Digger*, a play of Maine sea-folk, by Jean Ashe.

*Hunger*, a tragedy of North Carolina farm folk, by Ella Mae Daniel.

*Traficante*, a play of Spanish Florida, by Maxeda von Hesse.

*The Girl with the White Sweater*, a fantasy of the Carolina mountains, by Margaret Siceloff.

*Where There Is Faith*, a sophisticated play of an unsophisticated girl, by Kathleen Krahenbuhl.

*Concealed Aim*, a drama of a small-town bank, by Carl W. Dennis.

*The Passer-By*, a play of Carolina village folk, by Ralph Lyerly.

*Ancient Heritage*, a drama of a New England family, by Philip Goddard Parker.

*Octagon Soap*, a Carolina country comedy, by Nancy Lawlor.

*Damned Idealist*, a college drama, by Charles A. Poe.

*Rations*, a mountain folk comedy, by Catherine Threlkeld.

*Confidentially Speaking*, a satire on true-story writing, by Wilbur Dorsett.

*Muddy Jordan Waters*, a tragedy of the Carolina mountains, by Mildred Moore.

*The Villain Gets the Girl*, a modern satire in the old style, by Charles A. Poe.

*Pensioner*, a play of contemporary social conditions, by Alice A. Truslow.

*The Devil's Trampin' Ground*, a tragedy of mixed blood, by Sara Seawell.

*Yours and Mine*, a comedy of domestic difficulties, by Ella Mae Daniel.

*I Sing Forever*, a tragedy of the North Carolina mountains, by Mildred Moore.

*The Settin' Up*, a country wake, by Sara Seawell.

*Tsalagi*, an historical drama of the Cherokee Indians, by Billy Greet.

*And So They Grew*, a play of little ladies, by Ellen Deppe.

*Wait a While*, the first act of a full-length domestic drama, by Kenneth Bartlett.

*Goldie*, a comedy of a Negro Saturday night, by Wilbur Dorsett.

*Crazy-Patch Quilt*, a play of the Carolina tobacco country, by Anne Hyman Moore.

*Ca'line*, a Carolina folk comedy, by Bernice Kelley Harris.

*Metropolitan Feodor*, a romantic drama of seventeenth-century Russia, by Philip Goddard Parker.

*So It Will Last*, an eighteenth century romance, by William Howard Wang.

*The Best Butter*, a modern tea-room comedy, by Joseph Lee Brown.

*Virtue*, a satiric interlude, by Leonard Rapport.

*Hangman's Noose*, a tragedy, by Charles A. Poe.

*Bathroom Echos*, or *The Tale of a Tub*, a slightly ribald farce of character, by Walter Terry.

*Dark Journey*, a drama of a farm family, by Virgil Jackson Lee.

*There Ain't No Escape*, a comedy of arrested courtship, by Ella Mae Daniel.

*Thou Thief!*, a play of small-town complacency, by Ralph Lyerly.

*Barn Trash*, a mountain mystery-comedy, by Mildred Moore.

*Penny-Wise*, a drama of misunderstanding, by Ellen Deppe.

*Queer New World*, a Negro comedy-comment, by Wilbur Dorsett.

*Debtor's Hall*, an historical incident of colonial Massachusetts, by Jean Ashe.

## 1935-1936

*The School Teacher*, a play of character conflict, by Kenneth E. Bartlett.

*The Jew*, a drama of the Inquisition, by William Howard Wang.

*Across the Tracks*, a play of Southern slums, by Frank Durham.

*Cockle Doody Doo*, a play of Carolina fisherfolk, by Patricia McMullan.

# PLAYS PRODUCED BY THE PLAYMAKERS, 1918-1944

*Hjemlengsel (Home Longing)*, a Norwegian folk play, by Gerd Bernhart.
*The Red Velvet Goat*, a tragedy of laughter and a comedy of tears, by Josephina Niggli.
*Take Your Choice*, a play of college liberalism, by George Starks.
*Black Sheep*, a tragedy of the color line, by Marjorie Usher.
*Election*, a play of politics in a small Texas town, by Mary Delaney.
*The Other Way*, a tragedy of indecision, by Lawrence Wismer.
*A Most Lamentable Comedy*, a true story, by Barbara A. Hilton.
*Horses and Mice*, a tragi-comedy of musical playmakers, by Joseph Lee Brown.
*With Onions*, an illogical play of social protest, by Frank Durham.
*There Is No Guilt*, a play of a pacifist who died, by William Howard Wang.
*Transient*, a play of homeless men, by Walter Spearman.
*The Eternal Comedy*, a play of adolescence, by Mary Delaney.
*Prairie Dust*, a play of the Dakota drought, by Gerd Bernhart.
*Raise a Tune, Sister*, a play of Carolina fisherfolk, by Patricia McMullan.
*Grandma's Bonnet*, a comedy of age, by June Hogan.
*Brownstone Front*, a modern domestic tragedy, by William Chichester.
*Soldadera (Soldier-Woman)*, a play of the Mexican Revolution, by Josephina Niggli.
*Awakening*, a play of disillusionment, by Eleanor Barker.
*An Orchid to You*, a comedy of sorority life, by Jean Walker.
*Cat Alley*, a college comedy, by Kenneth Bartlett.
*An Active's Pledge*, a play of college fraternity life, by William A. Barwick.
*Frame-Up*, a play of social protest, by Jane Henle.

*Azteca*, a tragedy of pre-Conquest Mexico, by Josephina Niggli.
*The Cry of Dolores*, the story of Mexican independence, by Josephina Niggli.
*Sunday Costs Five Pesos*, a Mexican folk comedy, by Josephina Niggli.
*Country Sunday*, a play of white justice, by Walter Spearman.
*Mob-Tide*, an anti-lynching play, by John Walker.
*Strike-Breaker*, a play of protest, by George Starks.
*So Spin the Norns*, a play of Norse gods, by Gerd Bernhart.
*Fire of the Lord*, a play of religious fanatics, by Frank Durham.
*Ocean Harvest*, a tragedy of Maine sea-folk, by Jean Ashe.

## 1936-1937

*Ugly Hands*, a tragedy of factory women, by Kate May Rutherford.
*And Things Happen*, a play of post-war shadows, by Don Watters.
*Waitin'*, a drama of southwest Virginia mountains, by William Peery.
*The Barren Year*, a tragedy of a South Carolina farm woman, by David Beaty.
*Tidal Wave*, a tragedy of the South Carolina low country, by Evelyn Snider.
*Cause Unknown*, a tragedy of modern youth, by John Walker.
*Who's Boss?*, a comedy of Negro farm life, by Lubin Leggette.
*Widening the Channel*, a play of piedmont Virginia, by Sally Wills Holland.
*Six Dollars*, a tragedy of youth, by Virginia Peyatt.
*Leavin's*, a legend of the Carolina mountains, by Janie Malloy Britt.
*In the Jungle*, a drama of the "Milk and Honey Route," by William Peery.
*The Steep Road*, by Joseph Feldman.
*Funeral Flowers for the Bride*, a comedy of the Blue Ridge Mountains, by Beverley DuBose Hamer.

## PIONEERING A PEOPLE'S THEATRE

*Mrs. Juliet,* an ironic essay, by David Beaty.
*Rosemary's for Remembrance,* a play from the legends of Old Lynnhaven, by Sally Wills Holland.
*Abide With Me,* a comedy of rural South Carolina, by Walter Spearman.
*The Sun Sets Early,* a play of a small college, by William Peery.
*Near a Spring,* a play of southern Indiana, by Kate May Rutherford.
*Thank Rotary,* a play of the Big Brother movement, by William Peery.
*Penguin Soup,* a Second Avenue nightmare, by Jean Ashe.
*Shattered Glass,* a play of a woman's frustration, by Marion Hartshorn.
*Long Sweetenin',* a comedy of the hill folk, by Janie Malloy Britt.
*Courtship at Eight,* a play of children's love triangles, by Charlotte Wright.
*By Any Other Name,* a racial tragedy, by Marion Hartshorn.
*From Sullen Earth,* a play of rural South Carolina, by Frank Durham.
*Earth Treading Stars,* a Travelers Aid incident, by Manuel Korn.
*The White Doe,* a legend of North Carolina Indians, by William Peery.
*Seventy Times Seven,* a Carolina folk play, by William Ivey Long.
*"A-Pinin' and A-Dyin',"* a mountain comedy, by Emily Polk Crow.
*The Ivory Shawl,* a folk play of south Alabama, by Kate Porter Lewis.
*Drought,* a tragedy of rural South Carolina, by Walter Spearman.
*Fightin' Time,* a comedy of southern Indiana, by Kate May Rutherford.
*Toujours Gai,* a modern tragedy, by Virginia La Rochelle.
*Barge Incident,* a play of the New York water-front, by Herb Meadow.
*Naughty Boy,* a New York suburban comedy, by William Chichester.
*The Good-Bye,* by Paul Green.

*Pair of Quilts,* a folk comedy of eastern North Carolina, by Bernice Kelley Harris.
*While Reporters Watched,* a Christmas Eve newspaper mystery, by Rose Peagler.
*Mary Marge,* a comedy of Carolina fisherfolk, by Ellen Deppe.
*One Man's House,* a play of a Canadian reformer, by Gwen Pharis.
*The Worm Turns,* a comedy of adolescent love, by Jean Brabham.
*Murder in the Snow,* a drama of old Montana, by Betty Smith and Robert Finch.
*Three Foolish Virgins,* a Carolina folk comedy, by Bernice Kelly Harris.
*This Is Villa,* a portrait of a Mexican general, by Josephina Niggli.
*Twilight Song,* a play of religious superstition, by Donald Muller.
*Kid Sister,* a comedy of adolescence, by Wieder Sievers.
*Pasque Flower,* a play of the Canadian prairie, by Gwen Pharis.

### 1937-1938

*The Cross of Cannair,* a social drama of New York in 1887, by Lynette Heldman.
*Uncle Smelicue,* a Carolina mountain comedy, by Lois Latham.
*This Side Jordan,* a play of farm life in the middle west, by Lynn Gault.
*It Don't Make No Difference,* a folk play of Tin Pan Alley, by Joseph Lee Brown.
*Hello, Hanging Dawg,* a Carolina mountain comedy, by Lois Latham.
*Kunstbeflissener (Student of Art),* a play of an artist's conflict, by Thad Jones.
*Pennies for Their Thoughts,* a domestic comedy of an author, by Noel Houston.
*Washed in De Blood,* a symphonic play of Negro life, by Rietta Winn Bailey.
*Hit's Man's Business,* a Carolina mountain play, by Lois Latham.
*And Darling, Do Be Tactful,* a domestic comedy, by Rose Peagler.

## PLAYS PRODUCED BY THE PLAYMAKERS, 1918-1944

*The Last Christmas*, a drama of death row, by Noel Houston.
*His Boon Companions*, a temperance comedy, by Lynn Gault.
*Where the Wind Blows Free*, a play of the Texas range, by Emily Polk Crow.
*Hidden Heart*, a comedy of Armenian-American folk, by Howard Richardson.
*Still Stands the House*, a drama of the Canadian frontier, by Gwen Pharis.
*Wings to Fly Away*, a Negro ritual drama, by Rietta Winn Bailey.
*Last Refuge*, an outlaw comes home, by Noel Houston.
*Chris Axelson, Blacksmith*, a folk comedy of western Canada, by Gwen Pharis.
*West from the Panhandle*, a tragedy of the Dust Bowl, by Clemon White and Betty Smith.
*Let the Chips Fall*, a comedy of domestic intrigue, by Emily Polk Crow.
*Fresh Widder*, a play of Colington Island fisherfolk, by Lacy Anderson.
*Stick 'Em Up*, a comedy of frontier New Mexico, by Gordon Clouser.
*Me an' De Lawd*, a Negro play of eastern North Carolina, by James Bunn Dowdy.
*Montana Night*, a drama of the old west, by Robert Finch and Betty Smith.
*Triflin' Ways*, a comedy of the Missouri Ozarks, by Lealon N. Jones.

### 1938-1939

*Uncle Spence Goes Modern*, a play of the North Carolina highlands, by William Wolff.
*The Long Ago*, a nostalgic Oklahoma comedy, by Noel Houston.
*Bad Yankees*, a boarding school comedy of Mississippi, by Antoinette Sparks.
*Wash Carver's Mouse Trap*, a Carolina mountain comedy, by Fred Koch, Jr.
*Swappin' Fever*, a comedy of the Missouri Ozarks, by Lealon N. Jones.
*Runaway*, a play of a reform school boy, by Dorothy Lewis.
*Design for Stella*, a comedy of Manhattan, by Sanford Stein.
*Old Man Taterbug*, a play for children, by Mary Louise Boylston.
*The Reticule*, a comedy of the reconstruction period, by Katherine Moran.
*According to Law*, a drama of an Oklahoma court, by Noel Houston.
*Out from New Bedford*, a play of the whaling days in old New Bedford, by Frederick G. Walsh.
*These Doggone Elections*, a comedy of the Great Smoky Mountains, by Fred Koch, Jr.
*Texas Forever*, a play of the revolt against Mexico, by Emily Polk Crow.
*Lipstick*, a comedy of college life, by Mary Hyde.
*Swamp Outlaw*, a drama of Henry Berry Lowrie, by Clare Johnson Marley.
*Store-Bought Teeth*, a comedy of the Kentucky mountains, by Marie Haass.

### 1939-1940

*Squaw Winter*, a play of a family in Maine, by Frances Langsdorf Fox.
*Got No Sorrow*, a Negro ritual drama of the Carolina low country, by Caroline Hart Crum.
*Strong Hands for Hurting*, a tragedy of piedmont North Carolina, by Edward Post.
*New Britches*, a comedy of western North Carolina, by Evelyn Dawn Matthews.
*Winter Parade*, a play of changing America, by Adrian Spies.
*Black Tassels*, a play of South Carolina Negro life, by Frank Guess.
*Whipplesnout*, a frog fantasy for children, by Mary Louise Boylston.
*Mist in the Hills*, a play of the Carolina highlands, by Evelyn Dawn Matthews.
*Torch in the Wind*, a drama of "Billy the Kid," by Chase Webb.
*Banked Fires*, a play of an apartment house janitor, by Constance Smith.
*The Devil's Bread*, a morality play, by Ed-

ward Post.

*Outside De Gate*, a Negro graveyard fantasy, by William Long.

*Mi Amigo*, a comedy of "Billy the Kid," by Chase Webb.

*Taffy, the Tiger*, a play for children, by Mary Louise Boylston.

*Come Spring*, a play of old age and relief, by William Long.

*The Woman from Merry River*, a folk fantasy with music, by Chase Webb.

*The Scarlet Petticoat*, a folk comedy of the black belt, by Kate Porter Lewis.

*Truth or Consequences*, a play of spring in New York City, by Constance Smith.

*Billy, The Kid*, by Chase Webb.

*Watermelon Time*, a folk comedy of the black belt, by Kate Porter Lewis.

*Three Links O' Chain*, a comedy of the Alabama black belt, by Kate Porter Lewis.

*Party Dress*, a tragedy of the Alabama backwoods, by Kate Porter Lewis.

*The House in Avondale*, a comedy of Birmingham aristocracy, by Kate Porter Lewis.

*June Bug*, a play about an ordinary family, by Lucy Crenshaw.

*Dark Bayou*, a play of Louisiana farm folk, by Laurraine Goreau.

*August Angel*, a play of "Big Meetin' Time," by Neil Hartley.

*Cozy Corners*, a farce of a women's hotel, by Katherine Hill.

*A Daughter to Marry*, a comedy of the Pennsylvania Amish, by Carl Bashore.

*Sho' Nuff Dead*, a Negro comedy, by Herbert Lee.

### 1940-1941

*Night Run*, a play of a bus trip, by Emilie Johnson.

*Sarah Baske*, a play of the Maine Coast, by Merle McKay.

*The Bridegroom Waits*, a comedy of the country, by Frank Guess.

*Sermon on a Monday*, a play of the democratic ideal, by Joseph D. Feldman.

*Nine-Hour Shift*, a play of the importance of reason, by Marian Maschin.

*Swing You Sinner*, a Negro play with music, by Tom Avera, Jr.

*Curse Me These People*, a play of the changing world, by Joe Salek.

*Too Much Paradise*, a folk play of Eden, by Sanford Stein.

*Uncertain Death*, a farce comedy, by William L. Maner, Jr.

*Parole*, a play of man's love of freedom, by Robert Bowers.

*The Wider Field*, a play of the Connecticut Valley, by Marian Maschin.

*Union Forever*, a play of the end of the War Between the States, by Mrs. A. R. Wilson.

*First Wave*, a comedy of refugees from Europe, by George Levy.

*Saint of the Lord*, a drama of rural life in eastern North Carolina, by Elton Parker.

*The Ninth Commandment*, a comedy of Victorian virtue, by W. T. Chichester.

*Fire Worshipper*, a play of a middle-western college, by Lelia Allen McMillan.

*Bridal Mist*, a romance of Hudson Valley folk, by Mary Brill.

*Hit's Bud's Army Now*, a Carolina mountain comedy, by Jane Elizabeth Morrow.

### 1941-1942

*Black Friday*, a play of Chicago middle-class life, by Barry Farnol.

*Her Star Has Moved*, a folk comedy of old Peking, by T'ang Wen Shun.

*Tarantula*, a play of the Copenhagen waterfront, by Kai Jurgensen.

*The Cross on the Door*, a tragedy of the invasion of Denmark, by Kai Jurgensen.

*A Man's Game*, a satirical comedy of diplomacy, by Robert Schenkkan.

*The Hand of Providence*, a play of Quaker life in Maine, by Selah Richmond.

# PLAYS PRODUCED BY THE PLAYMAKERS, 1918-1944

*The Red Oak*, a play of an Iowa farm, by Barry Farnol.
*The Wandering Dragon*, a folk tale of old China, by T'ang Wen Shun.
*The Vengeance of K'noh*, a legend of the Huron Indians, by McCurdy Burnet.
*Got No Misery*, a comedy of Negro superstition, by Genie Loaring-Clark.
*Pen in Hand*, a domestic dilemma, by Ellen Mary Pillsbury.
*A Motley Assembly*, an adaptation of an early American play by Mrs. Mercy Otis Warren, by Marion Gleason.
*Real Trouble*, a domestic comedy, by Ellen Mary Pillsbury.
*Boer Commando*, a play of the end of the Boer War, by Robert Schenkkan.
*Shee Shih, the Aching Heart*, a romance of ancient Cathay, by T'ang Wen Shun.
*Compound Fracture*, a comedy of women at war, by Charlotte Stephenson.
*The Toymaker*, a play of the Danish waterfront, by Kai Jurgensen.
*Androboras*, a political fantasy by Robert Hunter, Governor of New York; printed in New York, 1714. The first play published in America. Adapted by Marion Gleason.
*Flower Gold*, a play of the Montana Rockies, by Martha Knight.
*Flora Macdonald*, a play of the North Carolina Scottish heroine, by Clare J. Marley.
*The Candle Poppin'*, a comedy of the Kentucky mountains, by June Randolph.

## 1942-1943

*King in the Kitchen*, a musical fantasy, by Elaine Berg.
*De Lost John*, a Negro play of piedmont Carolina, by Walter Carroll.
*Pecos Bull*, an historical play of the Texas frontier, by Russell Rogers.
*Food and the Student*, a documentary radio script, by Wharton Black.
*The Sea Wall*, an interlude, by Elaine Mendes.
*God and the Bishop*, a comedy of Moravian customs, by Elizabeth Trotman.
*Park Bench Blitz*, a black-out, by Lucile Culbert.
*Tim-Berr!*, a tragedy of west coast loggers, by Doris Marsolais.
*Look Down, Look Down*, a tragedy of a Negro convict, by Walter Carroll.
*Give Us Time to Sing*, a vignette of the city, by David Hanig.
*Fleas and Figs*, an imaginative comedy of Syrian life, by Mary-Averett Seelye.
*My World to Grieve*, a drama of youth in wartime, by Walter Carroll.
*The Right and the Left*, an army blackout skit, by Marcelle Clarke.
*Back-Street Blues*, a play of Baltimore street life, by Walter Carroll.
*To the Young*, a comedy drama of today, by David Hanig.
*Never Miss a Trick*, a ghostly comedy, by Marion Gurney.
*There Must We Ever Be*, a drama of the war, by Anne Osterhout.
*Sackcloth and Sauerkraut*, a summer-time comedy, by Ellen Mary Pillsbury.
*Muddy Water*, a tragedy of river folk, by David Hardison, Jr.
*Sunday's Child*, a romantic comedy of a Methodist parsonage, by Elizabeth Welch.
*Crusoe Islanders*, a drama of primitive folk in the swamps of eastern North Carolina, by Clare J. Marley.
*Four in a Room*, a play of working girls in wartime Washington, by Sally Martin.

## 1943-1944

*There's Always Morning*, a drama of today, by David Hanig.
*Listen, My Children*, a play for tomorrow, by Tom Avera.
*Lovingly, Gay*, a wartime comedy, by Gwendolyn E. London.
*The Georgian Dandy*, a romance of colonial

## PIONEERING A PEOPLE'S THEATRE

Georgia, by Nananne Porcher and Carrington Cross.
*Wailers to the Wind*, a study in black and white, by Anne Bridges.
*Scuttlebutt*, a comedy of Midshipmen's School, by Tom Avera.
*The Valentine Princess*, a tale of hearts, by Elizabeth K. Solem.
*Strange Sun*, a tragedy of adjustment, by Paul Ramsey, Jr.
*Carnival Cantata*, a modern fable, by David Hanig.
*Harp Upon the Willows*, a drama of the homefront, by Staff Sergeant Harvey L. Hannah.
*Heaven Is What You Make It*, a folk play of the army camps, by Corporal Hyman Levy.
*Prologue*, a fantasy, by Corporal Robert E. Beck.
*Hotel Armageddon*, a fable of the last resort, by Carrington Cross.
*Thirty Minutes Out of Midnight*, a play in verse, by David Hanig.
*Morning Edition*, a comedy of the news behind tomorrow's headlines, by Kat Hill.
*The Wraith of Chimney Rock*, a legend of the Great Smoky Mountains, by Clare J. Marley.
*Divided We Stand*, a comedy of modern life, by Anne Osterhout.
*The Tale of a Tub*, a comedy of Texas school teachers, by Myrtle Phaye Proctor.
*Salt Sands*, a play of Ocracoke Island, North Carolina, by Virginia Page Spencer.
*Pilgrim's Rest*, a Georgia Negro comedy, by Jessie Daniel.

### 1944 (Fall)

*Big Meetin' Time*, a ritual-play of the Falconites, by Clare J. Marley.
*Unshielded Lamp*, a domestic play of today by David Hanig.
*Rich Man, Best Man*, a comedy of a Greek country wedding, by Mary T. Colones.
*The Distances to Go*, a drama of readjustment, by Anne Osterhout.
*Poor Mr. Burton*, a comedy-mystery, by Mary Brooks Popkins.
*Wings in the Sun*, a study of women who wait, by Mary Lou MacGowan.

### ORIGINAL FULL-LENGTH PLAYS

*Job's Kinfolks*, a play of the mill people, in three acts, by Loretto Carroll Bailey, November 7-8-9, 1929.
*Playthings*, a comedy of illusion in three acts, by Anthony Buttitta, February 28, 1931.
*Rest for My Soul*, a play in three acts, by Ann Wishart Braddy, May 28, 1931.
*Strike Song*, a new play of southern mill people, by Loretto Carroll Bailey, December 10-11-12, 1931.
*Snow White*, a children's play in two acts, by Sallie M. Ewing, May 26, 1932.
*Sad Words to Gay Music*, a new comedy in three acts, by Alvin Kerr, February 23-24-25, 1933.
*A House Divided*, a comedy-drama in three acts, by Frederica Frederick, May 8, 1934.
*Shroud My Body Down*, a folk dream, by Paul Green, December 7-8, 1934.
*Water*, a play of pioneer settlement in California, by Alton Williams, April 13, 1935.
*The Enchanted Maze*, by Paul Green, December 6-7 and 9, 1935.
*Singing Valley*, a comedy of Mexican village life, by Josephina Niggli, July 15, 1936.
*The Fair-God (Malinche)*, a new play of Maximilian of Mexico, by Josephina Niggli, December 3-4-5, 1936.
*Sharecropper*, a new Negro drama in five scenes, by Fred Howard, February 24-25-26, 1938.
*Smoky Mountain Road*, a comedy of the

## PLAYS PRODUCED BY THE PLAYMAKERS, 1918-1944

Carolina highlands, by Fred Koch, Jr., July 11-12-13, 1940.

*The Marauders*, a new play of contemporary Oklahoma, by Noel Houston, March 5-6-7-8, 1941.

*Remember Who You Are*, a new comedy of Southern manners, by Frank Guess, July 10-11-12, 1941.

*Cocky Doodler*, a new comedy of the South, by William Maner, Jr., July 8-9-10-11, 1942.

*Down to the Sea*, a new play of Danish fishermen, by Kai Jurgensen, March 3-4-5-6, 1943.

*The Twilight Zone*, a new play of Europe on the eve of invasion, by Tom Avera and Foster Fitz-Simons, March 9-10-11, 1944.

### FULL-LENGTH PROFESSIONAL PLAYS

#### 1919-1920
*The Importance of Being Earnest*, by Oscar Wilde.

#### 1922-1923
*Seventeen*, by Booth Tarkington.

#### 1925-1926
*The Torch-Bearers*, by George Kelly.
*Le Malade Imaginaire*, by Molière.

#### 1926-1927
*A Thousand Years Ago*, by Percy MacKaye.
*She Stoops to Conquer*, by Oliver Goldsmith.
*Le Barbier de Seville*, by Beaumarchais.

#### 1927-1928
*Ten Nights in a Bar-Room*, by William W. Pratt.
*You and I*, by Philip Barry.

#### 1928-1929
*The Dover Road*, by A. A. Milne.

#### 1929-1930
*The Show-Off*, by George Kelly.
*The Crocodile Chuckles*, by Elmer Greensfelder.

#### 1930-1931
*The Importance of Being Earnest*, by Oscar Wilde.
*East Lynn*, by Mrs. Henry Wood.
*The Perfect Alibi*, by A. A. Milne.
*The Taming of the Shrew*, by William Shakespeare.

#### 1931-1932
*Saturday's Children*, by Maxwell Anderson.
*A Doll's House*, by Henrik Ibsen.
*Cinderella*, by Harry Davis. (Junior Playmakers).
*The Butter and Egg Man*, by George S. Kaufman.

#### 1932-1933
*Uncle Tom's Cabin*, dramatized by George L. Aiken.
*You Never Can Tell*, by George Bernard Shaw.
*Ali Baba and the Forty Thieves*, by Harry Davis. (Junior Playmakers).

#### 1933-1934
*The House of Connelly*, by Paul Green.
*Princess Ida*, by W. S. Gilbert and Arthur Sullivan.
*The Witching Hour*, by Augustus Thomas.
*Wappin Wharf*, by Charles S. Brooks. (Junior Playmakers).
*Topaze* (in French), by M. Marcel Pagnol.
*Hay Fever*, by Noel Coward.
*The Cradle Song*, by G. Martinez Sierra.

#### 1934-1935
*R. U. R.*, by Karel Capek.
*The Young Idea*, by Noel Coward.

#### 1935-1936
*Three-Cornered Moon*, by Gertrude Tonkongy.
*Paths of Glory*, by Sidney Howard.
*La Porteuse de Pain* (in French), by Montepin and Donnay.

#### 1936-1937
*The Drunkard*, by W. H. Smith and A Gentleman.

## PIONEERING A PEOPLE'S THEATRE

*The Pirates of Penzance*, by W. S. Gilbert and Arthur Sullivan.
*Monsieur de Pourceaugnac*, by Molière.
*Personal Appearance*, by Lawrence Riley.

### 1937-1938

*Johnny Johnson*, by Paul Green.
*Boy Meets Girl*, by Bella and Samuel Spewack.
*La Tour de Nesle*, by Alexander Dumas *pere* et Frederic Gaillardet.
*Laburnum Grove*, by J. B. Priestley.
*The Blue Bird*, by Maurice Maeterlinck.

### 1938-1939

*Room Service*, by John Murray and Allen Boretz.
*The Sorcerer*, by W. S. Gilbert and Arthur Sullivan.
*Our Town*, by Thornton Wilder.
*Mr. Pim Passes By*, by A. A. Milne.

### 1939-1940

*No More Peace*, by Ernest Toller.
*The Highland Call*, by Paul Green.
*H.M.S. Pinafore*, by W. S. Gilbert and Arthur Sullivan.
*Kiss the Boys Good-Bye*, by Clare Booth.
*The Field God*, by Paul Green.
*Ah, Wilderness!*, by Eugene O'Neill.

### 1940-1941

*Love's Old Sweet Song*, by William Saroyan.
*The House of Connelly*, by Paul Green.
*Patience*, by W. S. Gilbert and Arthur Sullivan.
*Family Portrait*, by Lenore Coffee and William Joyce Cowen.

### 1941-1942

*The Male Animal*, by Elliott Nugent and James Thurber.
*Abe Lincoln in Illinois*, by Robert Sherwood.
*The Pirates of Penzance*, by W. S. Gilbert and Arthur Sullivan.
*George Washington Slept Here*, by Moss Hart and George S. Kaufman.

### 1942-1943

*Arsenic and Old Lace*, by Joseph Kesserling.
*The Eve of Saint Mark*, by Maxwell Anderson.
*Iolanthe*, by W. S. Gilbert and Arthur Sullivan.

### 1943-1944

*The Boss of Bar Z*, by Nelson Compston.
*Watch on the Rhine*, by Lillian Hellman.
*The Yeomen of the Guard*, by W. S. Gilbert and Arthur Sullivan.

### 1944 (Fall)

*The Skin of Our Teeth*, by Thornton Wilder.

## OUTDOOR PRODUCTIONS OF PROFESSIONAL PLAYS

*The Taming of the Shrew*, by William Shakespeare, July 31, 1919.
*Twelfth Night*, by William Shakespeare, July 29, 1920.
*Much Ado About Nothing*, by William Shakespeare, July 29, 1921.
*As You Like It*, by William Shakespeare, July 29, 1922.
*The Comedy of Errors*, by William Shakespeare, August 28, 1923.
*The Taming of the Shrew* (Tercentenary Production), by William Shakespeare, October 12, 1923.
*Prunella*, by Lawrence Housman and Granville Barker, May 30 and August 26, 1924.
*The Rivals* (Sesquicentennial Revival), by Richard Brinsley Sheridan, May 29-30, 1925.
*The Poor Little Rich Girl*, by Eleanor Gates, August 21, 1925.
*The Romancers*, by Edmond Rostand, May 28-29, 1926.
*A Thousand Years Ago*, by Percy MacKaye, August 24, 1926.

## PLAYS PRODUCED BY THE PLAYMAKERS, 1918-1944

*The Tempest,* by William Shakespeare, April 30 and May 1, 1928 (Benefit Shakespeare Memorial Theatre Fund).

*Rip Van Winkle,* as played by Joseph Jefferson, May 24-25, 1929.

*Agamemnon,* by Aeschylus, July 17, 1929.

*Romeo and Juliet,* by William Shakespeare, May 16-17, 1930.

*Alcestis,* by Euripides, July 11-12, 1932.

*A Midsummer Night's Dream,* by William Shakespeare, May 19-20, 1933.

*The Women Have Their Way,* by Joaquin and Serafin Alvarez Quintero, July 7, 1933.

*Hamlet,* by William Shakespeare, May 25 and 27, 1935.

*Iphigenia in Tauris,* by Euripides, July 16 and 19, 1935.

*Lysistrata,* by Aristophanes (Gilbert Seldes' Modern Version), May 22-23, 1936.

*Androcles and the Lion,* by George Bernard Shaw, May 21-22, 1937.

*The Merry Wives of Windsor,* by William Shakespeare, May 20-21 and 28, 1938.

*Noah,* by Andre Obey, May 18-20, 1939.

*The Cradle Song,* by G. Martinez Sierra, July 9, 1939. (Junior Playmakers).

*Peer Gynt,* by Henrik Ibsen, May 22-23-24, 1942.

*A Midsummer Night's Dream,* by William Shakespeare, May 14-15-16, 1943.

*The Winter's Tale,* by William Shakespeare, May 19-20-21, 1944.

### ONE-ACT PROFESSIONAL PLAYS

#### 1921-1922

*Suppressed Desires,* by Susan Glaspell and George Cram Cook.

*How He Lied to Her Husband,* by George Bernard Shaw.

#### 1929-1930

*Joe,* by Jane Dransfield.

*The Angel Intrudes,* by Floyd Dell.

*The Stronger,* by August Strindberg.

*Modesty,* by Paul Hervieu.

*The Man in the Bowler Hat,* by A. A. Milne.

*The Open Door,* by Alfred Sutro.

*The Man on the Kerb,* by Alfred Sutro.

*The Mayor and the Manicure,* by George Ade.

*Enter the Hero,* by Theresa Helburn.

*Dawn,* by Percival Wilde.

*Suppressed Desires,* by Susan Glaspell and George Cram Cook.

#### 1930-1931

*The Constant Lover,* by St. John Hankin.

*Mansions,* by Hildegard Flanner.

*Fancy Free,* by Stanley Houghton.

*The Rising of the Moon,* by Lady Gregory.

*Cocaine,* by Pendleton King.

*Suppressed Desires,* by Susan Glaspell and George Cram Cook.

*A Proposal under Difficulties,* by John Kendrick Bangs.

*The Chased Lady,* by Ruth Welty.

*The Boor,* by Anton Chekhov.

*Helena's Husband,* by Philip Moeller.

#### 1931-1932

*The Hand of Siva,* by Ben Hecht and Kenneth Sawyer.

*The Man on the Kerb,* by Alfred Sutro.

*Words and Music,* by Kenyon Nickolson.

*In the Morgue,* by Sada Cowan.

*The Open Door,* by Alfred Sutro.

*Things Is That-A-Way,* by E. P. Conkle.

*Rosalie,* by Max Maurey.

*The Man in the Stalls,* by Alfred Sutro.

*Tomorrow and Tomorrow* (Act II, Scene I), by Philip Barry.

*The Constant Lover,* by St. John Hankin.

#### 1932-1933

*The Stronger,* by August Strindberg.

#### 1933-1934

*The Proposal,* by Anton Chekhov.

*Rosalie,* by Max Maurey.

## PIONEERING A PEOPLE'S THEATRE

*Einer Muss Heiraten* (in German), by Alexander Wilhelmi.
*The House Across the Way,* by Katherine Kavanaugh.
*Modesty,* by Paul Hervieu.

**1934-1935**

*Le Crime d'un Cerveau Malade,* adapted by Walter Creech.

**1936-1937**

*The Twelve Pound Look,* by J. M. Barrie.
*The Flattering Word,* by George Kelly.
*The Boor,* by Anton Chekhov.
*Fin d'Apres-Midi d'automne,* adapted by Walter Creech.

**1938-1939**

*Funiculi Funicula,* by Rita Wellman.
*Dance of Death,* by W. H. Auden.

**1939-1940**

*Air Raid,* by Archibald MacLeish.
*Bury the Dead,* by Irwin Shaw.
*Salome,* by Oscar Wilde.
*L'Anglais Tel Qu'On le Parle,* by Tristan Bernard.

# Carolina Folk-Plays Published In Books

### Carolina Folk Plays

*First Series*

Edited with an introduction, "Folk-Play Making," by Frederick H. Koch, and containing five one-act plays by native authors. Five full-page illustrations from the original productions. (New York, Henry Holt and Company, 1922.)

*Second Series*

Edited with an introduction, "Making a Folk Theatre," by Frederick H. Koch, and containing five one-act plays by native authors. Seven full-page illustrations from the original productions. (New York, Henry Holt and Company, 1924.)

*Third Series*

Edited with an introduction, "The Carolina Playmaker," by Frederick H. Koch. Foreword by Paul Green. Containing six one-act plays by native authors. Six full-page illustrations from the original productions. (New York, Henry Holt and Company, 1928.)

### Carolina Folk Comedies

*Fourth Series*

Edited with an introduction, "Adventures in Playwriting," by Frederick H. Koch. Foreword by Archibald Henderson. Containing eight one-act plays by native authors. Eight full-page illustrations from the original productions. (New York, Samuel French, 1931.)

### The Lord's Will and Other Plays

By Paul Green, with an introduction by Frederick H. Koch. Illustrated from the original productions. (New York, Henry Holt and Company, 1925.)

## PIONEERING A PEOPLE'S THEATRE

### Lonesome Road
A volume of Negro plays by Paul Green. (New York, Robert McBride and Company, 1926.)

### American Folk Plays
Edited with an introduction, "American Folk Drama in the Making," by Frederick H. Koch. Foreword by Archibald Henderson. Containing twenty one-act plays by native authors from various states. Fifteen full-page illustrations from the original productions. (New York, D. Appleton-Century Company, 1939.)

### Mexican Folk Plays
By Josephina Niggli, edited with an introduction, "Playmaker of Mexico," by Frederick H. Koch. Foreword by Rodolfo Usigli. Containing five one-act plays and seven full-page illustrations from the original productions. (Chapel Hill, University of North Carolina Press, 1938.)

### Folk Plays of Eastern Carolina
By Bernice Kelly Harris, edited with an introduction, "Plays of a Country Neighborhood," by Frederick H. Koch. Containing seven one-act plays and nineteen full-page illustrations. (Chapel Hill, University of North Carolina Press, 1940.)

### Carolina Folk-Plays
Edited with an introduction, "The Carolina Playmakers," by Frederick H. Koch. Foreword by Paul Green. Containing *Carolina Folk-Plays, First, Second* and *Third Series*. (New York, Henry Holt and Company, 1941.)

### Alabama Folk Plays
By Kate Porter Lewis, edited with an introduction, "Plays of the Deep South," by Frederick H. Koch. Containing five one-act plays and illustrations from the original productions. (Chapel Hill, University of North Carolina Press, 1943.)

www.ingramcontent.com/pod-product-compliance
Lightning Source LLC
Chambersburg PA
CBHW081834300426
44116CB00014B/2586